The Narcissistic Family

The Narcissistic Family

Diagnosis and Treatment

Stephanie Donaldson-Pressman
Robert M. Pressman

JOSSEY-BASS
A Wiley Company
www.josseybass.com

Published by

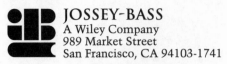

JOSSEY-BASS
A Wiley Company
989 Market Street
San Francisco, CA 94103-1741

www.josseybass.com

FIRST PAPERBACK EDITION PUBLISHED IN 1997.
THIS BOOK WAS ORIGINALLY PUBLISHED BY LEXINGTON BOOKS.

Jossey-Bass books and products are available through most bookstores. To contact Jossey-Bass directly, call (888) 378-2537, fax to (800) 605-2665, or visit our website at www.josseybass.com.

Substantial discounts on bulk quantities of Jossey-Bass books are available to corporations, professional associations, and other organizations. For details and discount information, contact the special sales department at Jossey-Bass.

We at Jossey-Bass strive to use the most environmentally sensitive paper stocks available to us. Our publications are printed on acid-free recycled stock whenever possible, and our paper always meets or exceeds minimum GPO and EPA requirements.

Library of Congress Cataloging-in-Publication Data

Donaldson-Pressman, Stephanie.
   The Narcissistic family : diagnosis and treatment / Stephanie Donaldson-Pressman, Robert M. Pressman. — 1st pbk. ed.
     p.   cm.
   This book was originally published by Lexington Books, 1994.
   Includes bibliographical references and index.
   ISBN: 0-02-925435-3. — ISBN 0-7879-0870-3 (pbk.)
   1. Adult children of dysfunctional families.   2. Narcissists—Family relationships.
3. Emotional deprivation.   I. Pressman, Robert M.   II. Title.
RC455.4.F3D66   1997
616.85'85.—dc21   97-16678

HB Printing   10 9 8 7 6 5 4 3
PB Printing   10 9 8

For Sarah, Rebecca, and Jonathan—
who are well loved

S.D.P.

For Henry Gilfond—uncle, author, mentor,
and keeper of the light.

R.M.P.

Contents

Acknowledgments

A number of individuals were both supportive and helpful in the production of this book. Susan F. Berman of the North Kingstown Library and Kenneth T. Morse of the University of Rhode Island Library were extremely generous in giving their time to locating source material. Nancy Lieberman was helpful in a thousand ways during the process, not the least of which was in keeping our offices running while we were involved with finalizing the manuscript. Carol Mayhew, in charge of production for Lexington/Macmillan, was knowledgeable, organized, and kind—all of which were much appreciated. We owe special thanks to Chris Kelly, whose intelligent and respectful copy editing was a delight as well as an education. Many of our patients were involved in both giving us feedback as the theory and techniques were in development, as well as in generously allowing us to use portions of their personal stories in the book; we are grateful. Our deepest appreciation, however, is for our editor and friend, Margaret Zusky, whose belief in the concept of the narcissistic family model made the book happen. Her comments and suggestions were invariably insightful, and her support was unwavering. Thank you, Margaret.

Introduction

The Focus

The Narcissistic Family is a book written by therapists for therapists. It is for those brave people who on a daily basis, engage patients in that mysterious, private, and sometimes beautiful struggle we call therapy.

The authors are two therapists who have worked in the trenches—the moderately comfortable, moderately soundproof rooms where hopeful patients and hopeful therapists are placed together for about an hour at a time. Like many therapists, we have struggled with patients who have been refractory to treatment. We look for books, workshops, and words of wisdom from our colleagues, with hopes of finding the answers as to why the impasses exist and how to overcome them.

The most helpful information for us is inevitably action oriented. The reasons and the theories are fine, but we want to know how to apply them—what to do behind those closed doors, how to help the client. This book puts forth a new viewpoint in working with a puzzling and difficult patient population. It does not give a new diagnostic category. However, it does suggest a common thread that ties together individuals who, depending on the day they are interviewed, might otherwise receive a diagnosis of a variety of personality disorders (borderline, overanxious, narcissistic, paranoid, and dependent) or clinical syndromes and disorders (multiple personality, dysthymic, and posttraumatic stress). Moreover, the narcissistic family model provides a framework for therapists within which they can help individuals who share this common thread.

A Broader View

Links between the experiences of childhood and their sometimes permanent effect on adult behavior have long fascinated observers of human behavior. Of particular interest has been the impact of one's family of origin on personal development. In the last decade, the concept of the "adult child of alcoholism" (ACOA) has helped us to understand the nearly predictable effects of being raised in an alcoholic family system. As therapists, many of us have worked for years with individuals suffering from what appeared to be immutable low self-esteem, inability to sustain intimacy, and/or blocked paths to self-understanding. The concept of the ACOA opened a new door to the understanding of such problems. Therapist/authors such as Woititz, Black, Gil, and Bradshaw (among others) have drawn vivid images of how children's personalities are molded in a special way by alcoholic families.[1] The literature produced on this topic has cleared a much wider path of recovery for children of alcoholic parents. It has also increased the sensitivity of therapists to the impact of alcoholic rearing on personality development. At one time, therapists seldom asked directly about the drinking patterns of the patient's parents; now such questions are routinely explored in initial assessment interviews.

Of late, a new body of literature has been created: books written by abuse survivors both to focus attention on the devastation caused by physical and sexual abuse and to give validation and guidance to other survivors, whether male or female. Laura Bass and Susan Davis have articulated the trauma of sexual abuse, as well as techniques helpful for recovery, in a landmark text, *The Courage to Heal*, while Stephen Grubman-Black was among the first to attack the myth of male invulnerability to sexual abuse in a poignant narrative, *Broken Boys/Mending Men*.[2] In fact, many bookstores now offer more self-help books for various types of survivors than they do for dieters, heretofore a staple of the paperback publishing industry.

Common Links

In our work at the Rhode Island Psychological Center, along with the benefits of working with the ACOA and abuse models came a puzzle. What about individuals who had the traits of an ACOA but whose parents did not drink, or rape, or beat? True, there was dysfunction in their families, but the common thread was elusive. Among adult children of dysfunctional (but nonalcoholic and nonabusive) families, we found a body of personality traits previously identified with the ACOA model. These included chronic depression, indecisiveness, and lack of self-confidence.

Within this population we found common behavioral traits as well: a chronic need to please; an inability to identify feelings, wants, and needs; and a need for constant validation. This group of patients felt that the bad things that happened to them were well deserved, while the good things that happened were probably mistakes or accidents. They had difficulty being assertive, privately feeling a pervasive sense of rage that they feared might surface. They felt like paper tigers—often very angry, but easily beaten down. Their interpersonal relationships were characterized by distrust and suspicion (bordering on paranoia), interspersed with often disastrous episodes of total and injudicious trusting and self-disclosure. They were chronically dissatisfied, but were fearful of being perceived as whiners or complainers if they expressed their true feelings. Many could hold their anger in for extremely long periods of time, then become explosive over relatively insignificant matters. They had a sense of emptiness and dissatisfaction with their achievements; this was found even among individuals who externally may have been viewed as very successful. The list of people included professionals who were obsessively involved in their enterprises, but were unable to achieve at a level at which they found satisfaction. In relationships, these individuals frequently found themselves in repeated dead-end situations.

Because these symptoms were so well defined in the popular literature about adult children of alcoholism, we asked some individuals from nonalcoholic dysfunctional families to read such books as *Adult Children of Alcoholics* by Janet Woititz and *Outgrowing the Pain* by Eliana Gil.[3] The clients returned, identifying somewhat with the syndrome, but not at all with the examples of drunk or brutal parents. Some things about the model rang true—denial of feelings, a sense of emptiness, recurrent ineffective patterns of personal inter-action—but not enough to be very helpful.

Working the Old System

We did two things to deal with the discrepancies between the examples of "causes" of ACOA-abuse personality traits and the actual experiences of our clients. First, when reading the self-help literature, we asked clients of nonalcoholic/nonabusive families to substitute the word *dysfunctional* for *alcoholic* or *abusive*. Second, we assured those clients whose childhood memories were still vague that the books we recommended would be helpful, even if their personal experiences did not seem fully to fit the descriptions given.

The substitutions and assurances helped. Meanwhile, perhaps in recognition of how terms such as *adult children of alcoholism* (or *abuse*) were too narrow, the literature began to change. Variations of terms that did not limit themselves by referring to a specific dysfunction (for example, '*adult children*') began to appear. The same question, however, kept returning: what really goes on in these families that causes those common psychological problems we used to label as ACOA traits? The principle clue was that in the absence of alcohol abuse, other forms of dysfunctional parenting (such as incest, physical abuse, emotional neglect and physical absence) seemed to produce the same symptoms.

An Emerging Viewpoint

As we began to track common traits shared by the parent systems of the survivors, we identified a pattern of interaction that we labeled the *narcissistic family*. Regardless of the presence or absence of identifiable abuse, we found one pervasive trait present in all of these families: *the needs of the parent system took precedence over the needs of the children.*

We have found that in the narcissistic family, the needs of the children are not only secondary to those of the parent(s), but are often seriously *problematic* for the latter. If one is to track the narcissistic family on any of the well-known developmental scales (such as Maslow's or Erikson's), one sees that the most fundamental needs of the child, those of trust and safety, are not met.[4] *Furthermore, the responsibility of needs fulfillment shifts from the parent to the child.*

In this family situation, the child must be reactive to the needs of the parent, rather than the converse. In fact, the narcissistic family is consumed with dealing with the emotional needs of the parent system.

In the narcissistic family, children are recruited in the process of satisfying the parents' needs. Where the father is cocaine addicted, both the spouse and the children dance around the father so as not to induce conflict. Where the mother is "borderline," there is a similar dance performed by the spouse and the children. In the incestuous family, the children are unprotected from the victimizer, who is not confronted by the spouse. The spouse of the troubled parent puts energy into sustaining the status quo and mollifying his or her partner, to the detriment of the children.

In the narcissistic family, the child's behavior is evaluated not in terms of what it says about what he or she may be feeling or experiencing, but in terms of its impact on the parent system. For example, in a healthy family, a child's receiving an 'F' on a report card alerts the parents to the presence of a problem. This situation is then examined in terms of the child's needs and development: is the work too hard, is the child under stress, does he need help, tutoring, support, or the like? In the narcissistic family, though, the same problem is examined on the basis of difficulty presented for the parent: is the child disobedient, lazy, embarrassing, or just looking for excessive attention?

In this example, the healthy family would react by expressing concern for the feelings of the child and presenting his 'F' not as a personal failure, but as a problem to be solved. In the narcissistic family, however, the reactions of the parent(s) indicate to the child that his feelings are of limited or no import. The child does not *have* a problem, he *is* a problem. To go one step further, the child does not have a need (the treatment of dyslexia, anxiety, developmental delay, depression, and so forth) but rather is a label (lazy, stupid, class clown, screwup, or something similar). The consequences of the child's actions on the parent(s) are of primary importance.

Over time, these children learn that their feelings are of little or negative value. They begin to detach from their feelings, to lose touch with them. Often this denial of feelings is functional to the child, as to express them only adds fuel to the fire. *Instead of understanding, recognizing, and validating their own needs, these children develop an exaggerated sense of their impact on the needs of their par-*

ent(s). Indeed, they become the reflection of their parents' emotional needs. The needs of the parent become a moving target on which they struggle to focus. Because they feel responsible for correcting the situation without having the requisite power and control to do so, the children develop a sense of failure. Moreover, they fail to learn how to validate their own feelings and meet their own needs. In time, the children undergo a semipermanent numbing of feelings. As adults, these individuals may not know what they feel, except for varying degrees of despair, frustration, and dissatisfaction.

The road to recovery, which is mapped out in Chapter Four, is delineated in five separate stages. This involves the patients' understanding that they were not responsible for the parent system's actions in childhood, nor could they control them. It also involves, however, their understanding that, in adulthood, they have the power to control their recovery and are indeed responsible for it. In other words, *a child from a dysfunctional family is molded by the family's dysfunction, but-as an adult-no longer needs to be defined by it.*

Why Case Examples?

The book is peppered with case examples (as opposed to case studies). Our feeling was that after spending hours with their own patients, practitioners might not wish to plow through transcripts of sessions with others as a means of gleaning a few concepts. Therefore the examples are abridged but authentic vignettes, with the identifying information sanitized to protect confidentiality. To accommodate different scenarios and to make the text more readable, we have varied the authors' "voice" from time to time (referring alternately to "we," "I," and "the therapist"). Likewise in the presentation of case examples, we have varied the pronouns "he," "she," and "they," to make the text flow more smoothly.

We have also avoided using extreme scenarios whenever possible. Worst-case scenarios are relatively easy to understand: if a patient was maliciously boiled in a hot tub by his or her parents, it is not difficult to understand why emotional scars exist. We have found, however, that the histories presented by patients are usually more subtle. It is not necessary to be severely abused to receive trauma. We have observed individuals whose family of origin history was not dramatic, but who were nonetheless seriously affected. These individuals came from narcissistic families, where the dysfunction was pervasive yet covert.

These vignettes are meant to serve as mnemonic devices—hooks to which concepts may be attached. The cases were chosen to highlight different nuances of dysfunctional behavior within narcissistic families, which can range from patently obvious to confusingly subtle. As in nature, where elements seldom exist in a pure form—oxygen, for example, is found mixed with dozens of other substances in a product we call air—so it is with family traits. Although we may reference an incestuous or an alcohol-troubled family, dysfunctional upbringings seldom are presented by the patient in such pure form; rather, problems tend to be multidimensional. The case examples will help the therapist recognize key elements of the narcissistic family, even in its more covert forms.

Laying the Framework

We consider psychotherapy to be a healing art, a mixture of techniques, strategies, and personal alchemy designed to bring relief to and augment growth of the client.[5] To the scientifically minded, this orientation may smack of folkism or a loose, anecdotal process. There are, of course, disorders for which empirical evidence has supported one type of treatment over another: for example, in the treatment of simple phobias, the behavioral intervention of pairing successive approximations with reciprocal inhibition is purported to work in more than 90 percent of all cases.[6] Regrettably, the literature has few such successful pairings of treatment strategies with recognizable disorders. Psychology and social work are soft sciences, indeed.

And yet those of us in the field continue to search, to read, to go to workshops, to talk to fellow clinicians, to seek supervision—all with the hope of better helping our clients. For better or worse, our treatment methods seldom come under scrutiny (with the possible exception of insurance review). Mostly, we experiment—or muddle though—hopeful of finding techniques that fit our own personality and the needs of our clients.

Certainly there is a need for validation of treatment modalities. In the formulation of the null hypothesis, the researcher must first have a working framework, an orientation or direction to be explored. The presentation of the narcissistic family is the laying down of such a framework; it is the development and the implementation of this hypothetical model that has been helpful to the authors in working with a specific patient population. The framework includes: (1) a hypothesis of symptom formation and behavior sequelae, and (2) suggestions for treatment strategies. It does not contain—nor does it purport to consist of—frank validation studies of the same.

From our perspective, this book has two principal strengths. First, it postulates a broader (and possibly less mysterious) cause of a familiar grouping of symptoms once narrowly reserved for adult children of alcoholism, then expanded to children of dysfunctional families. In so doing it offers a theory to explain why so many individuals have similar symptoms, although their backgrounds may look very different, and yet be devoid of identifiable abuse. Second, the book provides a formula for dealing therapeutically with this population. The authors have detailed strategies that they have found beneficial in working with a population sometimes considered refractory to treatment.

In conclusion, the authors are setting forth a hands-on, action-oriented, therapist-directed treatment model. Although positive regard, validation, and support of the patient are critical aspects of the therapy, the therapist—within this model—is a proactive force in the process. While we are not presenting this model as a "new theory for the study of the self" (to use Kohut's terminology), we are suggesting that it presents the possibility for a starting point in the formulation of such a theory.[7] We believe the narcissistic family treatment model to be a necessary step forward in the evolution of the therapeutic process.

Part I
The Narcissistic Family Model

1
Narcissus and Echo:
The Original Narcissistic System

The mythological character of Narcissus has come to epitomize the concept of destructive self-love. There is another character in the legend, however, whom we often forget: Echo. And it is the relationship of these two characters from which we derived the name *narcissistic family* for our model.

In the legend, Echo has lost the ability to form her own words and can only repeat the utterances of others. When she falls in love with Narcissus she follows him, hoping that he will say some kind or loving words that she can then repeat back to him. When he says "I love you" to his own reflection, Echo is finally able to say it, too—but Narcissus is so taken with himself that he is unable to hear her.[1]

The story, of course, ends with the demise of both characters. Narcissus pines away beside the pool; his love of and absorption with his reflection in the water ultimately resulting in his death. Echo, unable ever to succeed in capturing the attention or love of Narcissus, goes into what appears to be a vegetative depression—lacking the will or inclination to eat or drink—and also dies.

The story of Narcissus and Echo is one of self-love that precludes the ability to see, hear, or react to the needs of another. Without too much of a stretch, it stands as a poignant allegory for the interactive relationships of the narcissistic family.

Narcissus represents the parent system, which is, for whatever reason (job stress, alcoholism, drug abuse, mental illness, physical disability, lack of parenting skills), primarily involved in getting its own needs met. Echo is the child, trying to gain attention and approval by becoming a reactive reflection of her parents' needs, thus never developing the ability to find her own "voice"—that is, to recognize her own wants and needs and develop strategies for getting them met. Within the narcissistic family system, the locus for meeting emotional needs becomes reversed: where the parents in a healthy family system attempt to provide for the emotional needs of the children, in a narcissistic family system, it becomes the responsibility of the children to meet the emotional needs of the parents.

Elements of a Narcissistic System

Skewed Responsibility

In a healthy family situation, parents accept responsibility for meeting a variety of their children's needs; they get their own needs met by themselves, each other, and/or other suitable adults. In such a family, the intrinsic expectation is that the children are *not* responsible for meeting the needs of their parents. Rather, children are "responsible" for gradually learning how to meet their own needs in an independent manner. The children, with their parents' support, are expected to be involved in an eighteen-year (more or less) process of learning how to care for themselves. If this process works properly, the children will also learn, through modeling, how then to be parents who can take care of their own emotional needs and meet the needs of their own children. In the words of Bradshaw:

> What a child needs most is a firm but understanding caretaker, who needs to be getting her own needs met through her spouse. Such a caretaker needs to have resolved the issues in her own source relationships, and needs to have a sense of self-responsibility. When this is the case, such a caretaker can be available to the child and provide what the child needs.[2]

In a narcissistic family the responsibility for the meeting of emotional needs becomes skewed—instead of resting with the parents, the responsibility shifts to the child. The child becomes inappropriately responsible for meeting parental needs and in so doing is deprived of opportunities for necessary experimentation and growth.

Reactive/Reflective

As Echo could only reflect the words of others, so children raised in narcissistic families become reactive and reflective individuals. Because they learn early on that their primary job is to meet parental needs—whatever those may be—they do not develop trust in their own feelings and judgments. As a matter of fact, their own feelings are a source of discomfort: it is better not to have feelings at all than to have feelings that cannot be expressed or validated.

Thus, rather than act on her own feelings in a proactive way, the child waits to see what others expect or need and then reacts to those expectations. The reaction can be either positive or negative—the child can elect either to meet the expressed or implied needs or to rebel against the needs—but either course of action is reactive.

In the same way, the child becomes a reflection of parental expectations. This happens in all families to some extent, of course; the concept of mirroring in personality/ego development is a long-established tenet of psychology.[3] Frequently in the narcissistic family, however, the mirror may reflect the child's inability to meet parental needs. This reflection almost always is interpreted by the child as inadequacy and failure on her part.

Problems with Intimacy

For the child of a Narcissistic family, intimate relationships are a problem. Children of these families have learned not to trust. Therefore in adulthood, as much as they may want to form close and loving relationships, they have difficulty letting down the barriers to trust they have erected.

The need for psychological and physical safety as essential building blocks for the development of trust is an elementary stage described in most developmental psychological systems (including those of Erikson and Maslow).[4] The survivor in a narcissistic family system often learns not to trust or unlearns trust, rather than never learns to trust. As infants and young children, many survivors were fed well, kept warm, and cuddled and nurtured. A needy, dependent infant (as all are) may pose minimal threat to the parent system: the needs are simple, and the parent system is able—and willing—to meet them. As the child grows and seeks to differentiate from the parent, however, his needs become more complex. The parent system may be frankly unable to tend to these needs, or it may be threatened by them and become increasingly resentful. At this point the responsibility for meeting needs begins to shift from parent to child, and the erosion of trust starts.

While certain overt behaviors (getting drunk and embarrassing the child, for instance) will obviously produce a crisis of trust for the child, adults raised in narcissistic families frequently describe more covert dysfunction, describing their parent(s) as "just there." Consider the case of Beth:

> **Beth's Story.** My mom was always there, doing the usual mom stuff. We had a lot of time in the house with her—she was . . . there. But I remember feeling like I couldn't get close enough to her. It's hard to describe. Like she was there, and she cared, but not really. . . . I remember telling her this big thing about my best friend humiliating me in the school cafeteria—in front of everyone—and she'd nod, and make all the right noises, but it was like she was putting in her time, doing the "mom thing" from the "mom book" . . . because as soon as I was finished, she'd start talking about Dad, about how pissed she was at him for something—like I'd never said my stuff at all! . . . And this wasn't one time, one incident—it was *All* the time! . . . I worshipped her; I guess I still do. . . . I know she loved me, but it was like trying to grab smoke—you see it, but you can't get it into your hand. I still feel that way.

Beth's story is not of overt or dramatic abuse. It is about the emotional unavailability of the parent. Beth sensed that her mother's focus was *not on Beth*, and she was right: it was on the relationship with her own husband. Beth's mother really wanted Beth to pay attention to her, to be her ally and to meet her emotional needs.

Narcissistic Family Systems

Often the narcissistic family system is difficult to understand for both the therapist and the survivor. Many cases illustrate rather dramatically abusive families that obviously conform to the model and would appear to be relatively easy to diagnose. There are a number of examples of these *overtly* narcissistic families in this book. Families dealing with drug and alcohol abuse, incest, and assaultive behaviors are all types of narcissistic families, but we, as therapists, have given them their own labels (the incest family, alcohol-troubled families, and so forth).

There are an equal number of case studies presented here dealing with *covertly* narcissistic families, however, in which the dysfunction is much more subtle. All therapists have had cases where patients are really troubled and have a lot of those traits we identify as ACOA behaviors, but we just cannot get a handle on where or why the problems started. There was no overt abuse; nobody drank or took drugs. The family actually functioned very well. Children got fed, were clothed, had birthday parties, took family trips, and graduated from good schools. The family looked normal, even on close inspection.

The problem was that the children were expected to meet the parents' needs. It was subtle, and it looked healthy, but it was not emotionally healthy for the child. The children from these families are the adults who come into therapy having read all the books, talked endlessly to their siblings and friends (all of whom have reinforced the idea that there was nothing wrong with the family), and thoroughly convinced themselves that there is something deficient or defective about their very core. There must be—there was *nothing wrong* with the way they were brought up!

The narcissistic family treatment model addresses the needs of this population, as well as of the survivors of more overtly abusive families. It is our hope that this modality will fill the existing void for dealing with a whole range of patients/clients who have never fit into any specific category—for whom there has not been a framework around which to organize treatment, or workable techniques to help therapists in their delivery of treatment to the Beth's and Becky's and Ben's of the world.

Becky's Story.   Becky is a thirty-one-year-old executive secretary for a high-level corporate executive. She is happily married and has three school-age children; the fourth and youngest child died at the age of sixteen months after a bout of pneumonia, six years prior to the onset of Becky's therapy. She entered therapy after living secretly with panic attacks for two years. She felt that she was at risk for suicide if she could not get help with the attacks.

Becky's accounts of her family-of-origin experience were those of a person who had come from a close, warm, religious family. There were six children; the father was a high-ranking military officer, and the mother stayed home and devoted herself to the children. Becky talked about always having lots of kids to play with, about her mom never minding that her house was the center of neighborhood play. She had memories of feeling special because they lived on military bases, and everyone saluted her father and watched out for the kids. She remembered being five or six and getting lost on the base, only to be "rescued" by six soldiers who took her for cocoa and doughnuts before driving her home in a jeep. She talked about going to her father's office and feeling terribly important because she was "the colonel's little girl."

When questioned about her relationships with her mother and father, however, her voice developed an edge. There was barely suppressed anger, even in the retelling of happy events. Becky came across as an armadillo—someone with a very hard outer shell protecting a soft and vulnerable core. Her comments about her family, her coworkers, and her husband were often sarcastic. She made caustic jokes about everything, her anger masquerading as humor. But over many months of therapy, a picture began to emerge. It emerged with agonizing slowness, as it was difficult for Becky to say anything about her parents that might be construed as negative.

Becky had, essentially, no emotional connection with her mother; her mother wouldn't permit it. Her mother was a "human doing (as opposed to human being).[5] More than a year into therapy, Becky described her as follows: "Mom spent all her time earning those f—-ing wings [referring to her mother's strong religious beliefs, especially in the afterlife]. Everything was about how it looked on the outside—there was no substance to any of our relationships. I remember all of us, perfectly dressed, lined up for church. The colonel's family, all eight of us, always in the same pew. If you were *dying*, you got up, got dressed, and went to church! She was so busy doing the right thing, and making sure we all did the right things, to ensure her place in Heaven. It didn't matter what we felt—or if we felt anything at all! It just mattered what we *did*! I, personally, always felt like crap—unless I was with my dad. He made me feel important. He was a hero. You know—the uniform, all those medals, people saluting him wherever we went. But my mom, boy, I just knew I didn't measure up. I didn't know why; I couldn't ask. I was cocky on the outside, but I was always angry, and . . . hurt.

As Becky's family-of-origin story progressed, it became apparent to her that the children's needs were not callously ignored, but rather were sacrificed to serve other (and, to her parents, more important) needs. Her mother's religious convictions made feelings irrelevant; there was a proscribed way to live, and that was how you lived—period. It did not matter how you felt about it. The father's career was also very important to both parents.

Becky's father was the primary focus of her mother's life. In this parent dyad, anything that threatened the father's status, ego, or peace of mind was intolerable. This was the unspoken dynamic that drove this narcissistic family. When Becky became pregnant at sixteen, her father became enraged and knocked her down a flight of stairs; her mother supported his actions, putting the blame on Becky. A number of years later, when Becky's youngest child died, her father was unable to attend the funeral—he claimed to be too upset. The day after the baby's funeral, Becky's mother told her that she was behaving selfishly for crying, that she had to "pick herself up and do the right thing" (which was clean the house and prepare a meal in case people stopped by). Whereupon Becky's mother left her, her distraught young husband, and their three small children to fend for them-selves; she went home, saying, "Your father needs me—this has been so hard on him."

"What about *me?*" Becky screamed in recounting the story. "Didn't she think it was hard on me? No—I wasn't allowed to feel, to grieve. I didn't exist for her, if I wasn't doing the right thing! God forbid I should cry, or hurt, or need them!"

With the exception of the one time when Becky's father pushed her, no one in this family was ever beaten. No one ever "did without" materially. Neither parent suffered from substance abuse, major mental illness, or physical disability. But it was a narcissistic family: the clear expectation was that the children would meet the parents' emotional needs, and that the children would not call upon their parents for emotional support.

Conclusion

The narcissistic family often resembles the proverbial shiny red apple with a worm inside: it looks great, until you bite into it and discover the worm. The rest of the apple may be just fine, but you've lost your appetite.

In the narcissistic family, most of what happens can be "just fine," but the emotional underpinnings are not there. The children are not getting their emotional needs met, because the parents are not focused on meeting them. Instead of providing a supportive, nurtur-ing, reality-based mirror for their children, narcissistic parents pre-sent a mirror that reflects their own needs and expect their children to react to those needs. The focus is skewed, and the children grow up feeling defective, wrong, to blame.

When one is raised unable to trust in the stability, safety, and equity of one's world, one is raised to distrust one's own feelings, perceptions, and worth. When one is raised as a reactive/reflective being—as an Echo—one has not been taught the skills necessary to live a satisfying life.

2
Characteristics
of the Narcissistic Family

In the narcissistic family, the needs of the parent system are paramount. Whether it is composed of two natural parents, one natural parent and one stepparent, a single parent, a single parent and significant other, a single parent and other relative(s), foster parents, grandparents, or any other imaginable configuration, the parent system's ability—or, more accurately, inability—to focus on the needs of the child or children is the determining factor in defining a narcissistic family. In Chapter One, we alluded to two categories of narcissistic families: overt and covert. Since all narcissistic families fall into one of these two categories, we open our discussion with a view of each.

Overtly Narcissistic Families

Overtly narcissistic families are relatively easy for the therapist to recognize, as they are the classic "dysfunctional" families. These families are characterized by parent systems that are involved with alcohol or drugs, physically or sexually abusive, criminal, overtly mentally ill (with a history of institutionalizations or disabling depression, for example), and/or profoundly neglectful. (A more indepth discussion of implications for treatment of adults raised in traumatically abusive narcissistic families is found in Chapter Eight.)

In these families, the parent system is so overwhelmingly self-involved that it may have difficulty meeting even lower-level needs (food, clothing, shelter, and safety). The child born into the overtly narcissistic family becomes reactive/reflective very early in life—often from infancy, or from the onset of the profound parent system dysfunction.

The Family Secret

Perhaps the single outstanding feature of these families is the *family secret*. In order to meet the parents' spoken or unspoken need, the children keep the abuse or neglect a secret from outsiders and, often, from each other. Rather than banding together for support, the children in these families are often isolated from each other. The "secret" is too scary to be discussed, even among themselves.

In therapy, adults raised in overtly narcissistic families may have very few childhood memories. Statements such as the following are common when these persons are questioned about their families of origin:

> "I really don't remember too much about it. It was a pretty normal family, I guess. I mean, we got punished if we did something wrong; Dad'd take the belt to us. But we deserved it." This was an early therapy statement from Ben, who was viciously beaten with regularity by his father from early childhood until mid-adolescence, when he became larger and stronger than his father. The emotional abuse from both parents continued, however, and was equally if not more destructive.

> "My father was kind of an asshole. But he didn't do too much to me; my brothers had it much worse. And my mother was really great; she's still my best friend. We had a lot of good times. I really don't remember a whole lot from then." This was an early therapy statement from Eileen, whose alcoholic father beat all the children while the mother looked on. The father was particularly verbally abusive to Eileen and singled her out for sadistic punishments, such as shooting her dog and then putting the dog's collar on the

pillow beside her head while she slept. When Eileen would try to talk to her mother about the beatings—particularly those of her younger brother, which were nearly fatal—her mother would silence her, saying, "You'll only make it worse." When Eileen tried to call the police during one incident, her mother unplugged the phone.

"There's no point in talking about my childhood. It was perfectly normal. Actually, I can't really remember anything about it; isn't that awful? But it was good." This was an early therapy statement from Kristen, whose father was a metropolitan policeman. He was continually absent, and when he was home, he was drunk. Her mother was chronically depressed and was institutionalized for long periods of time, during which Kristen—the only girl of four children—took over the housework, meal preparation, and care of her baby brother (born when she was ten). This pattern continued until she left home at nineteen.

"I was kind of a bad girl," Eleanor said bravely, trying not to cry but obviously overcome with embarrassment at having to admit her perceived "badness" to her therapist. "I don't know how my poor parents put up with me. I was quite a handful, I can tell you! But do we have to go into all that? I really don't have many memories. Anyway, I'm here to deal with my anxiety attacks, not my childhood! That's all over and done with." Eleanor's emotionally disturbed mother periodically battered her throughout her adolescence and was constantly accusing her, from about the age of ten, of being sexually promiscuous, calling her "slut" and "whore" in front of her "good" younger sisters. In reality, Eleanor was a highly moral youngster who remained a virgin until her marriage at nineteen.

The term *overtly narcissistic* is used to describe what the therapist perceives, not what the patient perceives. The patient who can readily identify the reality of his or her upbringing is the exception, not the rule. The typical adult from a narcissistic family is filled with unacknowledged anger, feels like a hollow person, feels inadequate and defective, suffers from periodic anxiety and depression, and has no clue about how he or she got that way.

Tension and Fear of Abandonment

Tension is the hallmark of the overtly narcissistic family. The children are all trying desperately to get attention and approval, and/or not to "rock the boat" and make things worse, in order to inject some control over the situation and make things better. The children's fear of abandonment causes them to go to extreme measures to deny—to other people, and often to themselves—the reality of their home situation. This fear of abandonment often carries over into adult life, making family-of-origin disclosures difficult and painful in therapy.

Covertly Narcissistic Families

The covertly narcissistic family is harder to recognize, as the dysfunctional behaviors of the parent system are more subtle. We can recall many instances of reviewing a patient's quite normal-appearing case history multiple times, looking for the abusive behavior that—based on the patient's symptoms—we felt *had* to be there. But it was not. During a case review at one staff meeting, a colleague, after giving a beautifully detailed summary of a difficult case, declared in frustration, "Who was the alcoholic? I *know* that someone in this family had a drinking problem!" But no one did. The problem was that the patient manifested all the symptoms we have associated with the alcohol-troubled family, without any evidence of familial alcohol or drug abuse; without, in fact, evidence of any kind of familial abuse. As the King of Siam said to Anna, "'Tis a puzzlement."[1]

The solution to the puzzle was often that the patient came from a covertly narcissistic family. This type of family looks just fine from the outside, and it looks pretty good from the inside, too. In fact, survivors of these families are absolutely mystified at the suggestion that any of their problems could stem from their family of origin. After all, nobody drank or took drugs, nobody hit anybody, nobody had a severe mental illness, and so on. Dad may have been a nine-to-five type, Mom a homemaker who baked cookies for the PTA. There were simply no problems.

In therapy, however, it will become apparent that the needs of the parents were the focus of the family, and that the children were in some way expected to meet those needs. Obviously, if the children are expected to meet parental needs, then they are *not* getting their own needs met, or learning how to express their needs and feelings appropriately. Quite the contrary: what the children are learning is how to mask their feelings, how to pretend to feel things they do not feel, and how to keep from experiencing their real feelings. Becky in Chapter One was an example of this.

Brad's Story.   "We won't get too far by talking about my family; they invented the word *normal* for my family," said Brad, a boyishly attractive thirty-one-year-old executive. Brad had entered therapy because of his inability to sustain relationships with women. Brad was a very successful busi-nessman who exuded confidence and enthusiasm; his low self-esteem was successfully masked in the business world. He devoted the bulk of his waking hours to his work. This had contributed positively to his rapid rise through the cor-porate ranks, but negatively to his interpersonal relation-ships. His workaholism, initially a defense against bad relationships, now made developing *any* relationship a problem.

Brad came from the prototypical covertly narcissistic family. His parents were both schoolteachers and active in the community. Brad and his sister were good students, tal-ented in athletics and music, and popular with their class-mates. The parents were home when the kids were home, the family ate dinner together six nights a week, and nobody overdrank, did drugs, smoked, swore, or hit any-body. They were apple-pie normal, on both the outside and inside.

"I used to wonder why I was so scared, why I felt so inad-equate," Brad said. "I looked at other kids' families—I mean, *really* looked. Ours wasn't different. It was normal. I mean, my parents had their fights, and stuff like that. But nothing excessive. The opposite, really. Neither of them would let you say anything bad about the other one! Mom could be a little overbearing at times, critical. But it was a loving family, and they always said how important the family was. It was good. It was just me. It still is; I can't stand to go back there. They don't really seem to mind, though."

When asked if his parents ever tried to talk to Brad about his feelings, his response was: "No, not that I can remember. Nobody talked about feelings. You just knew what you were supposed to do. If you didn't do it, you got in trouble. Maybe they talked about feelings with Betsy [his sister]; she was the really good one."

Brad's sister, who was two and a half years older than Brad, was a professional musician. Though they had been close in childhood, demanding jobs on opposite coasts had eroded their relationship. During the course of therapy, Brad was encouraged to get back in touch with his sister in order to find out her impressions about their upbringing. He was astonished to learn that she had childhood feelings very similar to his. Moreover, her perceptions were stronger. The following excerpts from a letter she wrote to him illustrate this: "I always felt that Mom and Dad had another agenda. . . . They were so taken up with each other that we didn't matter. . . . They were obsessed or jealous of each other, sexually. I remember *not* talking about feelings when I wanted to. It was as if the emotional tension between the two of them was so strong, they couldn't bear for us to be anything but cardboard cutouts of successful children. It was tense all the time in that house. I couldn't wait to graduate and go away to college."

When Brad received the letter from his sister, he was able to look at his family through new eyes, and he saw that her perceptions were accurate. Although he did not know why, he did agree that things went along okay in the house until one of the children made emotional demands on the parents. Then it got very tense. He said he learned to "always act happy." Brad and his sister learned to meet their parents' needs, and not to make demands for emotional support from their parents. In short, they came from a covertly narcissistic family.

Later in this chapter you will read Trisha's story. Trisha's family of origin is another good example of a covertly narcissistic family. There was no physical or sexual abuse, all of Tricia's physical needs were well met, and she was not exposed to inappropriate drug or alcohol use, inappropriate sexuality, or violence. The parental "dance" just did not include Trisha. At about the age of seven, she became unable to meet her parents' needs, and they were unwilling to meet hers.

A Matter of Degree

Whether covert or overt, the degree of a family's dysfunction may vary not only in an absolute sense but also in regard to specific children within the family. Patients come from families ranging from apple-pie normal to extremely peculiar, and even in the most peculiar ones, the children's needs and feelings may be considered important, and the parents may do their best to meet them. Therefore, even if the family was sometimes unstable or chaotic, the children will have a good sense of themselves and of their importance. They know that their feelings matter and that those feelings will be attended to, to the best of their parents' ability.

Conversely, we have all had patients who came from alcohol-troubled families (or some other kind of classically dysfunctional family) but who nonetheless are remarkably well put together. They have a fairly good sense of themselves and are able to choose suitable mates, be nurturing parents, and have close friendships and meaningful careers. Families with some degree of dysfunction may produce one child who does very well while the other siblings are a mess, psychologically speaking. Why does one child seem to escape relatively unscathed? We postulate that this child got his or her needs met to a greater degree than his or her siblings.

We know that no two siblings grow up in exactly the same environment; parents respond differently to each child, with the response based on the personalities of both parents and child. One child may have the same weird sense of humor as the mother, one may share Dad's love of fishing, and a third may be a great cuddler. How the parents relate to these three children will differ because the children themselves are different, and because the parents' feelings (about themselves, primarily) during different interactions also vary. It is therefore possible that one child in a family may get his or her emotional needs met on a fairly consistent basis while the others do not.

One patient who had switched therapists (because of a geographic relocation) commented that her previous therapist had said on more than one occasion, "I understand how your sisters turned out to be the way they are [alcoholic, with alcoholic husbands]; what I don't understand is how you turned out so well!" The answer was that although the patient and her sisters had grown up in a narcissistic family, the degree to which their needs were met varied greatly.

Issues of Trust

There are characteristics we have found in most narcissistic families that provide ways of looking at the families and identifying key areas of relationship dynamics. Trust—and the evolution of distrust—is the most salient.

We have found that survivors of narcissistic families have difficulties with trust, but not necessarily because their elementary needs went unmet in infancy. On the contrary, many survivors of covertly narcissistic families appear to have been well nurtured in infancy and to have had both physical and psychological needs met in a healthy way for the first twelve to twenty-four months of life (and longer for some.) At least a rudimentary level of trust would, therefore, have been established at that time.[2]

As discussed in Chapter One, the problems in narcissistic families often begin as the children attempt to assert themselves and make emotional demands on their parent system.[3] The parent system may be frankly unable to tend to these needs, and it may be resentful or threatened by them. As noted earlier, then, the child learns not to trust, or unlearns trust, rather than never learns to trust.

Trisha's Story. Trisha's father was a much-decorated military officer, and her mother was an efficient and devoted military wife. When Trisha was a young child, she remembers her family as being "perfect. It was the perfect family. Daddy was the handsome Naval officer, Mother was the beautiful and elegant wife, and I was the adorable baby. Life was an endless succession of garden parties and teas, with me being the center of attention. They took me everywhere with them. People always said I was 'like a little doll.' I thought my whole life would be like that—all cuddles and praise and laughter. When I look back on it, I could cry; it was so lovely. I have never felt so loved since."

As Trisha grew older, however, the family situation changed. "I remember feeling it when I was seven. I woke up in a panic. I went into the bathroom and stared at myself in the mirror. I was trying to figure out what was different about me—why I was wrong. What had I done to make my parents not love me anymore? I cried and cried. I couldn't figure it out. The next day, I decided that it was because I was bigger [her mother was petite, with a 'perfect' figure], so I decided not to eat. Daddy was in Vietnam at the time, so it was just the two of us—Mother and me. Mother didn't notice that I wasn't eating, but she didn't change toward me, either. She was very busy, always. We were living in Virginia to be near my grandparents. It was very social, and Mother loved it. When people would come over, Mother would dress me and tell me what to say. She never seemed pleased with me, even though I tried very hard to be cute. Mother and Daddy had always said I was 'so cute, so adorable', so I tried harder to do what I had always done. Now my Mother just said, 'act your age, Trisha!' or made some other comment that showed her disdain. She would send me upstairs to my room almost as soon as the people got there, and the maid would be with me. I just felt in the way and ugly.

"When Daddy came home, I knew that things would be like they were before, but they weren't. Suddenly he seemed irritated by me, too. He told Mother that I looked sick, and she took me to a doctor. He [the doctor] gave me some medicine, and I had to drink some milkshake-like things three times a day. Daddy enrolled me in gymnastics to 'shape you up,' and my mother got very angry at me if I wouldn't eat. She wanted to please Daddy, I guess. I started eating again; it wasn't worth the hassle to starve, and I kept growing anyway. But I was destroyed. I kept trying and trying to get them to love me like they had before, to be my Mommy and Daddy again, to be the 'me' I had been before . . ."

Here Trisha became very tearful. "Anyway, that's when I started pulling out my eyelashes. . . . When I got older, I acted out a lot. I did everything I could think of to get their attention—any attention, I didn't care. By then I was really pretty, and they didn't seem to mind having me at their par-

ties any more. But—I couldn't trust them. As much as I wanted their approval—I desperately wanted their approval—I
was afraid of it. I'd had it once, and lost it. So I did a lot of
stuff to hurt them—embarrass them. I was very promiscuous,
and I went out of my way to seduce young officers in
Daddy's command. The ultimate, 'Look at me! Screw you!' I
guess. I've never trusted anyone. Especially myself."

As Trisha moved through adolescence and early adulthood, her difficulties with trust pushed her into many damaging relationships and patterns. She had an overwhelming
need for male attention and approval, which, once achieved,
became too scary, so she would precipitate the end of the
relationship. She hated and distrusted women, and had no
female friends. (A focus of initial therapy was her ability to
deal with a female therapist.) She had discovered a satisfying
form of self-mutilation in early adolescence (pulling out of
all facial hair with tweezers) and, in spite of the cosmetic difficulties it presented, maintained the behavior until it was
now a deep-seated compulsion.

Obviously there are a number of factors present in Trisha's case.
Her family-of-origin story, however, is a good example of a narcissistic family where the child initially meets the parents' needs and so
has her own needs met in return. (See "The Inverted Parenting
Model," below.) It was good for her father's career, which was also
her mother's career, for the pair to be seen as a beautiful young couple with a beautiful baby. As the baby grew, however—got tall and
awkward, made more demands, and had schedules of her own to
follow—she was no longer viewed as an asset by her parents. While
Trisha's physical needs were attended to by a series of maids, her
emotional needs were attended to by no one. Her mother became
increasingly cruel and verbally abusive, her father alternately
cold/distant and warm/flirtatious.[4]

Trisha related that there were times, though, when for some reason her parents felt a need to "parent" and would suddenly and
inexplicably draw her in and shower her with attention and affec-
tion. This intermittent and unpredictable reinforcement is common
among narcissistic families; it keeps the children "hooked in" to the
parents in hopes of being able to precipitate a repeat performance,

while making them even more distrustful of themselves (for their perceived lack of ability to cause more positive interactions) and of others ("They suck me in and then drop me, so I won't let myself get sucked in").

The Inverted Parenting Model

As the child grows, the parents' own identity may become more and more involved with the child's development.[5] Simultaneously, as the child's needs become both more complicated and better articulated, he or she may start to infringe more obviously on the parent system. A cranky infant who demands parental attention at an inconvenient time can, after all, be placed in a crib with the door shut. An irate and tearful nine-year-old is an entirely different matter.

As the child's psychological needs become more of a factor in the life of the family, the narcissistic family truly develops. The parent system is unable to adapt to meet the child's needs, and the child, in order to survive, must be the one to adapt. The inversion process starts: the responsibility for meeting needs gradually shifts from the parent to the child. Whereas in infancy the parents may have met the needs of the child, now the child is more and more attempting to meet the needs of the parent, for only in this way can the former gain attention, acceptance, and approval.

In infancy, the baby's normal development is often rewarding to—and therefore rewarded by—the parents. For instance, the baby's smiles (gas or not!) are usually a source of pleasure for the parents and are greeted with excited voices, attention, cuddles. Eating, sitting up, movement, noises and attempts at vocalization are all usually both rewarding and rewarded. The child's needs and the parents' needs are in sync; there is no problem.

The youngster's normal development, however, may pose a threat to the parents. The toddler's exploration requires vigilance and patience; her shouts of "No!" and "Mine!" can be infuriating and embarrassing. The preschooler's questions and demands are intrusive and time-consuming. Further, *the needs of children—especially the emotional needs—increase geometrically as their tractability decreases.* As a normal child develops, her need to please herself and her friends increases as her need to please her parents decreases.

In a healthy family, however annoying this fact of life may be, it

still does not change the basic conceptualization of parental responsibility: the parents' job is to meet the child's needs, not vice versa.
In the narcissistic family, though, as the child's need for differentiation and fulfillment of emotional needs escalates with normal development, so does the parents' belief that their child is intentionally
thwarting them, becoming increasingly selfish, and so forth. The
parents, feeling threatened, thus "dig in their heels" and expect the
child more and more to meet parental needs.[6] Somewhere between
infancy and adolescence, the parents lose the focus (if they ever had
it) and stop seeing the child as a discrete individual with feelings and
needs to be validated and met.

The child becomes, instead, an extension of the parents. Normal
emotional growth is seen as selfish or deficient, and this is what the
parents mirror to the child. For the child to get approval, she must
meet a spoken or unspoken need of the parent; approval is contin-
gent on the child meeting the parent system's needs.

Lynne's Story.   Lynne was an honor student in her junior
year of high school, a likely candidate to be valedictorian of
her class and the recipient of many college scholarship
offers. Although an excellent and conscientious student, her
teachers were becoming concerned by her frequent absences,
tardiness, and changes in appearance and affect. Lynne could
be bright-eyed, on time, alert, and well groomed one day
and then an hour late, with uncombed hair and flat affect,
the next. Her weight also appeared to fluctuate erratically,
although it was difficult to tell as she usually wore loose,
dark-colored clothing. Her close friends were concerned
about her as well, and they confided in the school guidance
counselor that her mood swings and angry outbursts were
alienating her from most of her remaining friends. When
Lynne was approached by the guidance counselor, she
denied having any problems. Since Lynne's mother was an
employee of the same school district, the guidance counselor
felt that she would be reluctant to discuss any problems she
might be having out of loyalty to her mother, and so private
counseling was recommended.

When Lynne started in counseling, it was apparent that
she was determined to present a very together, adult, "in

charge" persona to the therapist. In just a few sessions, how-ever, the facade crumbled. Lynne was a desperately unhappy adolescent from a narcissistic family, but her loyalty to and feeling of responsibility for her mother was such that it was extremely painful for her to confide in anyone, including her therapist.

Lynne's parents were divorced when she was eight years old and her younger sister was five. Lynne's memories of her early childhood are scant. Mostly she remembered a rather passive father who was gentle with her but would get into screaming fights with her mother, who would then go to Lynne for comfort. Her personal experience with her father differed greatly from the negative picture her mother painted of him, which was confusing and unsettling for Lynne. When she would feel love for her father, "It made me feel bad—guilty, somehow. Like I was being disloyal to my mom."

Her mother presented herself to Lynne as someone constantly in need of reassurance, and her role was described as "more like a friend than a mother; we told each other every-thing." Lynne's mother dressed and, in many ways, acted like a teenager; her hair was worn as she had worn it in her teenage years (very long and straight), and she dressed in the same clothing worn by her daughters.

After the divorce, Lynne's role as confidante and emotion-al supporter escalated. In addition to being her mother's caretaker, she now assumed primary responsibility for her sister's care. While there was nothing inherently damaging about Lynne's taking on more responsibility at home so that her mother could go back to school, the emotional burden of constantly having to reassure her mother—that she was a good mother, a responsible person, someone who had done everything she could to hold her family together, attractive, young looking, not neglecting June (the younger child), and Lynne's best friend—made Lynne assume the role of parent to her mother. Lynne also felt a tremendous need to do everything she did without *looking* like she was doing much and without comment or complaint, so that her mother would not feel inadequate. Lynne gave up school trips because "Mom will be all alone" (June often spent weekends with their father; Lynne rarely did); she would not date if her mother was between boyfriends, so that Mom would not "feel bad."

By the time Lynne entered therapy, she was a seriously depressed adolescent flirting with bulimia and suicide in an unfortunate attempt to inject some control into her life. The job of parenting her mother had become too much for her.

Rules for Maintenance in Narcissistic Families

There are predictable means by which narcissistic family members relate to each other. These are the unspoken criteria by which the family is expected to operate. The purpose of the rules is to insulate the parents from the emotional needs of their children—to protect and hold intact the parent system. Therefore, all of these unspoken "rules for maintenance" of the narcissistic family system discourage open communication of feelings by the children and limit their access to the parents, while giving the parents unlimited access to the children.

Indirect Communication

In the narcissistic family direct, clear communication of feelings is discouraged. Individuals express their feelings obliquely. Requests are rarely direct; instead of "Sam, would you please set the table?" one gets "It would be nice if someone would set the table!"

When parents are upset or angry, they are usually unable to express those feelings in a timely and appropriate manner. One patient recalled that whenever her mother was angry with her father, the mother would be overly solicitous of the father at the dinner table and very critical of the children for their supposed lack of concern for their father's comfort: "Ed, pass your father the potatoes first. Stacy, give your father the butter *now* before his vegetables get cold." She would keep this up until the whole family was really anxious and uncomfortable and the meal was ruined, then would explode at some harmless remark made by the father and exit the table in tears. The father would stay at the table for a few minutes, then throw down his napkin and stalk out, leaving the children frightened, confused, and resentful. At no time were any of these incidents ever mentioned again or explained.

Triangularization

Another ineffective communication technique used in narcissistic families is triangularization. The parents communicate through a third party, usually a child. One patient, however, reported that her parents had for years communicated through the dog: "Buffy, tell your Daddy that Mommy wants to go out Saturday night." "Buffy, remind Mommy that Saturday is Daddy's bowling night." One day, Buffy decided to move out, and she took Daddy with her. The father even signed the dog's name to the note he left!

More commonly, however, the parents will "confide" in the child, with the implicit expectation that the child will carry the message to the other parent. The parents may also use the child as a buffer so that they do not ever have to communicate directly, planning their lives around the child (or children) and thus never being alone together; in other words, using the child as a defense against intimacy. In a third scenario, triangularization is employed by one parent to form an alliance with the child against another person—the concept of "the enemy of my enemy is my friend." This is confusing and damaging when the "enemy" is the child's other parent or a sibling.[7]

Again, such families are covertly narcissistic. It *looks* like the children's needs are being met, and they may indeed get a lot of time with one or both parents. The problem, of course, is that it is the parents' preoccupation with getting their own needs met that is driving the family relationships. The children cannot predict when or why good times will either happen or be withdrawn. They feel like they may have "gotten it right" when intimacy is encouraged, and "messed up" when it is discouraged. In reality they are not responsible for either their inclusion or exclusion from parental intimacy; it is their parents' own needs, and not the children's behavior, that is the motivation.

Lack of Parental Accessibility

Lack of parental accessibility refers to emotional accessibility—the ability to have conversations about feelings. Many survivors will say that they never had in-depth conversations with their parents. Their parents would "do work" for them (that is, transport them, provide for them, or buy things for them), but if they really wanted or needed to talk about their feelings, the conversation would quickly turn into an advice-giving session (do this, do that), a fight (you *should* have done this or that), or denial (you don't feel depressed, you're hungry and tired; things will be better in the morning). The parents were always "too busy" to talk. And, of course, the children could see that the parents *were* busy, doing things for the children, or the family, or the job. So, if the child felt resentful, it was because he was selfish, wrong, and mean-spirited.

Anna's Story.   Anna is a beautiful nineteen-year-old college student who models part-time. She entered therapy because of dysthymia and bulimia. Anna and her brother, Marshall, were eight and eleven years old, respectively, when their divorced mother decided to join the clergy. This necessitated six years of education, internship, and part-time jobs.

"I went from having a nice house with two parents, two cars, a dog, and a cat, to a kind of grungy apartment, no pets, no dad, and—essentially—no mom. I hated it. I didn't mind the apartment or the divorce—stuff like that; I had wanted them to get divorced, anyway. My brother and I both wanted that. My dad was a real scumbag; he fooled around on Mom and he was mean to us, so we were glad about the divorce. And the apartment was kind of neat, in a scruffy sort of way. But my brother and I, we sort of thought it would be like the three of us against the world; that Mom would be more available to us with Dad gone.

"After she had this big religious experience, she just changed. Overnight. That was bad enough. It was like living with a total stranger! Mom had been—not wild, but pretty cool after the divorce. I mean she went on a diet, let her hair grow, and started dating. Stuff like that. That was cool. She was still Mom, and my brother and I thought it was pretty funny. Like she was reliving her adolescence or something. But she was a great mother. She talked to us—really talked. We could tell her anything. Our friends loved her, too. Even though we were kind of poor after the divorce, it didn't make any difference. Our place was where all our friends hung out; they all loved Mom, and she loved them. That year was great. Then, like I said before, she got this religious thing, and she became a different person. Then she went back to school to become a priest, and suddenly I had no mother." (Anna became tearful as she said this.)

"She was always busy. With church stuff. And there were all these weird priests always around, having long, boring discussions that went on late into the night. I tried to wait up for them to leave so I could talk to her, but I'd fall asleep. Or cry myself to sleep. Then my brother started growing away from me. I understood. I mean, he was a teenager, and I was still a little kid. But it hurt—I was so alone. . . . Mom had God, and Marsh had his buddies and his girlfriend . . . and I had no one.

"Sometimes I'd try to talk to Mom, but she'd just say that she knew it was hard for me, that it was hard for her, too. That she missed me so much. Then she'd hug and kiss me and promise to spend time with me later. Ha! *She* missed *me*! That was rich! She didn't have to miss me—she could've been with me! A lot of the stuff she did—she didn't have to do it. It was not part of the program. She did it to look good.

"So, I was hurt and lonely. Angry, too, I guess. I started to develop when I was eleven, and by thirteen I was sexually active. I hated it! But at least (*Anna cries hard*) . . . at least someone would hold me and let me talk to them. I got pregnant and had an abortion when I was fourteen—two weeks before my mom was ordained."

"At the . . . ordination, she looked like a saint. Everybody said then—they tell me all the time still—how open she is, how easy to talk to . . . how caring she is. . . . I don't know. I can see it, I guess. That's what she is—to them. Everybody adores my mom. She does good. I know she does. But—how can you hate someone for doing God's work? I feel like such a bad person!"

Unclear Boundaries

In the narcissistic family, the children lack entitlement. They do not own their feelings; their feelings are not considered. When we do not have feelings, then others do not have to take our feelings into consideration.

Issues such as the right to privacy take on a different coloration in a narcissistic family. For instance, in a healthy family, privacy is respected and encouraged: parents do not come into bedrooms or bathrooms without knocking, they do not listen in on others' telephone conversations, read others' mail, or allow their own privacy to be abrogated by their children. There are clear boundaries, clear rules governing what the family members can expect from each other.

In the overtly narcissistic family, there may be no rules at all governing boundary issues such as privacy. Privacy may be a totally unfamiliar concept. People's possessions, time, and very bodies may be the property of a parent, caretaker, or stronger, more powerful sibling. In the house where the father is sexually abusing one or more of the children, for instance, the idea of privacy—private ownership—is ludicrous for the incest victim. If she does not own her body, she owns nothing and has no rights. There are no boundaries at all in terms of what she may expect or demand from others (nothing), and what others may expect or demand from her (anything).

In the covertly narcissistic family, there may be clear rules governing all manner of boundary issues, including physical privacy. The problem, however, is twofold. First, the rules may be broken by the parents as their needs dictate, and second, there are no boundaries in terms of emotional expectations for the children. The children are always expected to meet the parents' needs, but the needs of the children usually are met only by happy coincidence. (See "The Moving Target" below.)

Boundary issues are enormously complex for the survivor and thus are mentioned in many places in this text (see Chapter Six). Adults raised in narcissistic families often do not know that they can say no—that they have a right to limit what they will do for others, and that they do not have to be physically and emotionally accessible to anyone at any time. In their families of origin, they may not have had the right to say no, or to discriminate between reasonable and unreasonable requests. Children in narcissistic families do not learn how to set boundaries, because it is not in the parents' best interests to teach them: the children might use that skill to set boundaries with them! (See Janine's story in Chapter Four.)

The Moving Target

In the section above, it was mentioned that in the narcissistic family, the children may get their emotional needs met by accident—as a by-product of the parent system's getting its needs met. For example, Susie (age six) has a need to be nurtured. Susie's mother is usually "too busy" (it is irrelevant whether she is busy with Dad, cocaine, a job, or major depression—it feels the same to the children) to meet this need, and she demands that Susie's older sister, Joyce (age twelve) "get her out of my hair!" Susie does not get her needs for nurturance met by Mom; Joyce does not get her needs for either nurturance or autonomy met by Mom.

But suppose that the mother-in-law comes for a visit. Mom has needs for praise and esteem from her mother-in-law, who values good parenting. So, during the visit, Mom is available and cuddly to both her daughters. Susie and Joyce get their nurturance needs met, and Joyce gets some time free from baby-sitting and mothering her little sister. The mother-in-law praises Mom's parenting, so Mom gets her esteem needs met. Everybody is happy—temporarily. Mom met the children's needs, but only as an action *coincident* to getting her own needs met.

In the previous example, the effects are particularly damaging. The children may believe that they caused Mom to be more loving, which will encourage them to believe they have control over her actions. When Mom reverts to form, they may then believe that they have caused the rejection, too. They cannot win: they are taking responsibility for things they do not control. The only lesson they can learn from this pattern is that they have not gotten it right—yet. There is really something wrong with them; they got it right briefly, and then they blew it. The children will continue to try to hit the moving target—in this case, the "button" that causes their mother to nurture them.

Lack of Entitlement

The locus of difficulty, on which boundary setting, intimacy concerns, and virtually every other survivor issue is centered, has to do with emotional entitlement. In order to set boundaries with another person (whether it means saying no to sex, refusing to take an adolescent to the convenience store late at night to pick up a notebook for school because he "forgot" to ask earlier, or insisting on equal pay for equal work), one must know that one has the right to feel as one does: that one has the right to set the boundary, feel the feeling, or make the demand.

In narcissistic families, be they covert or overt, *the children are not entitled to have, express, or experience feelings that are unacceptable to the parents.* Children learn to do all manner of things with their feelings so as not to create problems for themselves vis-à-vis their parents: they stuff them, sublimate them, deny them, lie about them, fake them, and ultimately forget how to experience them. What has been extinguished in childhood—the right to feel—is difficult to call back in adulthood. But until adults understand that they have a right to feel whatever it is that they feel, and that they always *had* that right, they will be unable to move forward in boundary setting. And without appropriate boundaries, all relationships are skewed and unhealthy.

Mind Reading

Caroline, a young woman we treated, was one of those fairly well-put-together individuals referred to earlier in this chapter: the product of a narcissistic family who nonetheless managed to get many of her emotional needs met by her parents. Although Caroline's two older sisters were both alcoholic and dysfunctional, Caroline was happily married, the mother of two preschool children, and pursuing her master's degree part-time. Caroline would appear intermittently for issue-oriented therapy; in other words, from time to time circumstances would arise for which Caroline's upbringing had not sufficiently prepared her, and she would come in for two or three sessions to "get her head together," as she called it. One of these sessions had to do with mind reading.

Caroline's Story. Caroline had been raised in a narcissistic family where one of the unspoken rules was that her father was supposed to be able to intuit her mother's wishes without her mother's needing to verbalize them. If her father guessed right, everything was peachy. If her father guessed wrong (which was more often the case), however, there was hell to pay! Caroline remembered her father asking her mother what she wanted for Christmas, and her mother responding sweetly, "Why, don't be silly. Christmas is for children! Don't get me anything." So her father would get her mother nothing, or a few little things, and her mother would act hurt and angry for days. The same pattern occurred at birthdays and anniversaries. Her mother would also get upset if she got dressed up and her husband did not compliment her on her appearance. Caroline remembered asking her mother why she did not just tell Dad that she wanted him to tell her that she looked pretty—that it was important to her for him to notice and comment on her appearance. Caroline has never forgotten her mother's reply: *"If you have to ask for it, it loses its value."*

Caroline internalized that message from very early in her life, and it became an integral part of her worldview. If someone had to be told what she wanted, than the gift (of words, presents, or presence) had no value. If someone could not read her mind accurately, then there was no purpose in expressing her needs and wishes. So much for the merits of assertive communication.

The expectation that one's spouse or child should be able to read one's mind and meet every unspoken need is one of the more damaging "rules" in narcissistic families. It virtually assures that no one's needs will ever be met: I will not get what I want, and you will be a failure because you did not provide it. This is truly a lose-lose scenario. In families where mind reading is a requisite in interpersonal relations, the word *should* is used a lot ("he *should* have known that I needed him home; he *should* have noticed that I never wear blue")

The other maddening thing about the need to read minds is that it frequently occurs in spite of real protestations to the contrary. Remember Caroline's mother insisting that she wanted no presents, when in reality she did? The messages were complex in the extreme: not only are you to read my mind and come up with the real message, but in so doing you are also sometimes to disregard my expressed preferences. And it is up to you to figure out when to read my mind, and when to honor my explicit expressions of preference.

Caroline's mother used this ineffective communication

technique (which Caroline later labeled "the joys of martyr-dom") in a variety of circumstances, some with serious out-comes. Caroline remembers her mother's absolute demand, upon finding out that she needed an emergency hysterecto-my, that her father not cancel his plans to participate in a member-guest golf tournament to which he had already invited an out-of-town guest. Caroline has vivid memories of her father's assertions that he did not want to be golfing while his wife was in surgery, and of her mother's continuing insistence that everyone's life was not to be disrupted just because she was going into the hospital. Her father finally acceded to her expressed wishes. Caroline (who was then sixteen) dates the observable deterioration of her parents' relationship to this point in time. She maintains that her mother never forgave her father for not dropping out of the tournament, and that the atmosphere in the house was "tense and sad" from then on.

Conclusion

While the case vignettes presented in this chapter range from rela-tively benign to overtly abusive, the one thread connecting them has to do with skewed responsibility. Somehow, at some point in the families' histories, the responsibility for the meeting of emotional needs shifted from the parents—where it belonged—to the children. The children then become like those trees one sometimes sees in the forest: the trunk grows straight up for a while, and then for some reason (for example, lack of sun, encroachment by another tree, or storm damage) abruptly starts growing off to one side. Like those trees, at some point for children in narcissistic families their healthy emotional growth becomes arrested. Their feelings get turned off, and they start to grow in a different, unhealthy direction.

3

Narcissus, Narcissism, and the Narcissistic Family Model

This text is about individuals raised in a narcissistic family system. It is not about individuals who suffer from narcissistic personality disorder. Although it is possible that one (or both) parents in a narcissistic family system may have this or some other personality disorder, it is unlikely; personality disorders in the general population are not that common, and cases of narcissistic personality disorder, while apparently on the rise, still constitute a minuscule percentage of the therapeutic population.[1]

We use the term *narcissistic* in our treatment model more in a descriptive, rather than clinical, sense. In this respect our brand of narcissism is a child of Ovid, but a cousin of Freud as well. Narcissism implies self-absorption, lack of genuine caring, a certain superficiality, concern with external appearances, shallowness, distancing—an unwillingness to get too close or to give too much. Any or all of these descriptions, in varying degrees and with varying frequency, could be used to describe the parent system in a narcissistic family. Although these terms can also be used in the description of narcissistic personality disorder, there they are the tip of the iceberg. When the layperson uses the term *narcissistic* in a pejorative way—as in "That narcissistic little twit! All she ever thinks about is herself!"—he is really transposing narcissism for solipsism: the view that the self is all that exists, can be known, or has importance. He might more accurately say, "That solipsistic little twit!"

We are not categorizing individuals in a narcissistic family system as "pathological narcissists";[2] nonetheless, the definition of the system itself has parallels with the psychoanalytic framework that defines narcissism. At some points in the discussion of this model, psychoanalytic theory is cited; there is, in fact, so much to be gained from some understanding of the psychoanalytic evolution of the theory of narcissism that we have included a brief overview of that theory's development (from Freud through Kernberg and Kohut) in Appendix A. Our reference to psychoanalytic theory comes out of an appreciation for the historical basis of the narcissistic family model, as well as for the prior study and work done by others that contributes to the better understanding of our theory.

We recognize that narcissistic personality disorder, however, is a serious, often debilitating, inordinately painful condition that is extremely difficult to treat.[3] The primary proponents of psychoanalytic theory, with the exception of Heinz Kohut, have long endorsed psychoanalysis as the treatment of choice for narcissistic personality disorder. Even within that milieu, there are major disagreements concerning the efficacy and focus of differing treatment methods.[4] As our text unfolds, the reader will see that, for many reasons, we do not endorse psychoanalysis as a means of treating the disorders of individuals raised in narcissistic families.

Narcissus and Narcissism

To reference the disorder we label *narcissism* in any meaningful way, we must return to Ovid's telling of the myth:

> I burn with love of my own self; I both kindle the flames and suffer them. What shall I do? Shall I be wooed or woo? Why woo at all? What I desire, I have; the very abundance of my desires beggars me.[5]

In this version of the myth, Narcissus was the product of a rape. His mother, Liriope, a water-lady, was raped in a brook and nearly drowned. When Liriope asks a prophet about what her son's future will hold, and if he will live to old age, he answers, "If he ne'er know himself."[6] Narcissus, though physical beautiful and desired by many (of both sexes), remains aloof. He is loved and admired, especially by the tragic Echo, but he does not love or admire in return. At last, of course, he does find an object worthy of his love—his own reflection in a pool of water. He thus comes to "know himself," which results in his death. What remains is a beautiful white flower (the narcissus) that springs up beside the pool and is perpetually reflected in its waters.

There are many elements of this myth which have found their way into psychological studies and models (including our own): the story of Narcissus symbolically includes the perils of physical beauty, the pool as a mirror, rape, self-love, skewed self-esteem, homosexual love, perverse love, the role of empathy, water as life/death, and self-knowledge as death. That of Echo has been taken to represent reactive personality, an impaired sense of self, and lack of self-knowledge as death.

Perhaps more than any other mythological character, Narcissus has fascinated students of human behavior by dramatizing a host of characteralogic dualities: passion/coldness, aloofness/absorption, reality/illusion, insight/concreteness, unity/disunity, subject/object, and demanding/rejecting love. As Chessick so aptly points out, the term *narcissistic personality* has been used "with an astonishing variety of meanings, ranging from a sexual perversion to a concentration of psychological interest upon the self".[7] Therein lies the problem.

Narcissism Reborn

Havelock Ellis was the first student of psychology to incorporate the Narcissus myth into the body of psychological literature. Published at the end of the nineteenth century, "Auto-Erotism: A Psychological Study" (1898) described the loss of outward manifestations of sexuality to an internal "Narcissus-like" tendency to autoeroticism, often in dream activity. He linked the tendency toward sexual pleasure by one's self to totalitarian and perverse character.[8] During the same period, Paul Nacke described the attitude of one who treats his body as a sexual object, stroking and fondling himself as the primary outlet for his sexual drives; the term *Narcismus* (*Narzissismus*) was introduced by him to describe this activity as a sexual perversion.[9]

Freud first used the term *narcissistic* in 1910 as a footnote to his previously written *Three Essays on the Theory of Sexuality*.[10] While it was Rank (1911) who published the first psychoanalytic paper on the subject, it was Freud's 1914 essay "On Narcissism: An Introduction" that established the concept and terminology of what was to become a major focus of his developmental theory.[11] He also moved the study of narcissism away from sexual perversion, writing that "an allocation of the libido such as deserved to be described as narcissism might be present far more extensively, and that it might claim a place in the *regular* course of human sexual development" (italics added).[12]

Both Freud and Mahler viewed narcissism as conflict resolution, moving the infant from "primary" (healthy) narcissism, where the child knows (loves) only itself, into a successful transfer of love to an appropriate object (usually the mother).[13] Where this natural progression does not occur, or when trauma forces a child who has successfully made the transition from self-love to regress into primary narcissism, then the pathology we call narcissism or narcissistic personality disorder results.[14]

The Narcissistic Family Model

Although our paradigm parallels clinical narcissism, the name is derived from the relationship of Echo and Narcissus, and it is actually more concerned with Echo than with Narcissus. Instead of the narcissistic family model, we could have called it the parent-centered model, or even the Echo model—but there is, for most of us, an association with the word *narcissism* that is descriptively communicative. Further, there is an undeniable connection with psychoanalytic theory, particularly as exemplified by Freud's and Mahler's developmental theories.[15] Our model is indeed about a parent system that, for whatever reason, can mirror only itself and its own needs (Narcissus), and about a child who only exists for the parent to the extent that she meets or refuses to meet those needs (Echo). Although in a strict sense this model is not about pathological narcissism, it is about a system of relationships or interactions that bear qualities we commonly associate with narcissism: self-absorption, detachment, lack of empathy, the putting of the self (parent system) first, an exaggerated need for reassurance, and concern with external appearance over internal substance.

Theories do not spring up, full-blown, like Athena out of Zeus's forehead. The origins of the term *narcissistic family* are both historical and sociological. There are references throughout this book to both Ovid's and Freud's brands of narcissism to illustrate certain points or concepts. There are also many references to the concept of mental illness as a continuum. We can look at an individual's tendencies toward self-centeredness and grandiosity from a traditional object-relations perspective and make a diagnosis of narcissistic personality disorder, or we can assume the perspective that there is a degree of healthy narcissism that contributes to self-assertion, self-protection, and creativity. To borrow from Sheldon Bach:

> But that very self-centeredness which creates problems in object-relations may be necessary for exceptional creative capacity, and who is to say if grandiosity and fantasies of power may only appear pathological when unaccompanied by worldly success? Apparently, such distinctions are not always easy to make, and we cannot necessarily assume that healthy narcissists become darlings of the gods while only the unhealthy ones become patients.[16]

In order to illustrate our attitude that mental illness is largely in the eyes of the beholder—which is why the focus of this model is in the way people relate, and not their pathology—we would like to share a gem of a story from Cleckley's book *The Mask of Sanity*:

> A millionaire notable for his eccentricity had an older and better-balanced brother who, on numerous fitting occasions, exercised strong persuasion to bring him under psychiatric care. On receiving word that this wiser brother had been deserted immediately after the nuptial night by a famous lady of the theatre (on whom he had just settled a large fortune) and that the bride, furthermore, had, during the brief pseudoconnubial episode, remained stubbornly encased in tights, the younger hastened to dispatch this succinct and unanswerable telegram: WHO'S LOONEY NOW?[17]

A New Framework

In talking about the narcissistic family system, we are not describing individuals with chronic disorders. Instead we are talking about a new framework for (1) looking at the way people learned to interact in their families of origin, (2) analyzing the adult consequences of those childhood patterns of interaction, and (3) organizing strategies for dealing with those consequences in therapy. So, to the patient who needs to know "Who's looney now?" we answer nobody, or everybody; what difference does it make? This model is not about pathology, it is about acceptance (see Chapter Four)—acceptance of the realities of the past, and of the possibilities for productive change in the present.

Part II
Therapy with Adults
Raised in Narcissistic Families

4
Acceptance: The Key to Recovery

There are a number of concepts that are necessary for someone raised in a narcissistic family to master during the course of recovery. Within this model, however, none are more important than that of acceptance.

Acceptance does *not* imply resignation, or that things are okay as they are or were, or that one must necessarily hand things over to some "higher power."[1] In this model, it means a recognition and acceptance of *reality*: of how things really were in our family of origin, of the effects of that experience on our development, and that while as children we were not responsible for what happened to us then, as adults we are responsible for our own recovery now. As noted earlier, though we have been molded by our family-of-origin experience, we need no longer be defined by it.

Most patients are very concerned about having to "blame" their parents for deficits in parenting. They are afraid because they don't want to acknowledge their anger with their parents, and also because placing blame on their parents seems too easy—like a cop-out that eventually will backfire on them, and leave them feeling even more deficient than they do at present. Conversely, however, these individuals are more than ready to blame *themselves* for every-

49

thing—failed relationships, lack of job success, indecisiveness, their child's lack of coordination, the cake not rising, and so on. The concept that blame, in any form, may be irrelevant is often difficult for survivors to grasp. ("If I take it [blame] off me, don't I have to put it on someone else?" a patient once asked.)

Molten Gold

An example of how blame does not really have to be involved in the acceptance process is often helpful to patients. One we frequently use is that of molten gold: it can be poured into a mold for a bracelet or for a bedpan. The gold does not make the choice; it is not the gold's "fault" if it is molded into a bedpan instead of a bracelet.

So it is with children in narcissistic families. Regardless of intent, right or wrong, children get molded in certain ways. In order to understand and love oneself, it is important that one is able to see the reality of how one was molded. In childhood, one is molten gold. The potential for goodness and beauty is all there; it may be enhanced by one's upbringing, or it may be diminished.

In life the bedpan can be melted down, and the same molten gold can then be reformed into a bracelet that is a beautiful work of art. So it is with therapy: the adult, who has the control she lacked in childhood, can choose to see the reality of the past, let go of self-blame, and take the responsibility for reforming her present. Acceptance does not place blame or require forgiveness—it merely acknowledges the reality and places the potential and responsibility for healthy change on the survivor.

The Five Stages of Recovery

Working within the narcissistic family model, we have found that there are five stages through which patients must move in the process of recovery. Although they occur in a logical sequence, patients will swing back and forth among the stages. Nevertheless, being able to recognize, label, and explain the stages to the patient is an extremely useful tool for the therapist. Below we list the five stages, interspersed with presenting problems, recommended solutions, and case examples.

Stage One: Revisiting

In the first stage, the patient is able to remove the blinders and look at the reality of her childhood. This has to do with giving up the fantasies that the family has promulgated throughout the years. It means accepting that things were never ideal, that the child never had control, that things were never as good as the family pretended that they were. Further, it means that the individual can never recreate this "ideal" family of origin—because it in fact never existed. Continuing attempts to "get it right" (to create or recreate the ideal family) are a waste of time, because it cannot and will not happen. The patient as a child lacked the power to make it happen; she as an adult still lacks the power.

The Problem of Resistance. At this stage, most patients are reluctant to reframe their family-of-origin experience in terms of what actually happened, because it implies blame of the parent system and letting themselves [the patients] off "too easy." This process of revisiting the past requires constant therapeutic focusing on the reality of the past *as it affected the patient*; that regardless of how loving or well-meaning the parent system may have been—regardless of how much the survivor may now be able to look back and understand that his parents had a terrible childhood themselves, that there were awful financial problems, that mother was really mentally ill— the reality for the patient raised in the narcissistic family is that his parent(s) were unable to meet his emotional needs.

The concept of responsibility without blame is very difficult for many patients to grasp. This is one of the places in the therapeutic process where patients can get "stuck." They can seem to move past it and to be making real strides in therapy, and all of a sudden they are back into a recitation of the litany: it's all my parents' fault—I can't blame my parents—it's all a cop-out—I'm just defective-deficient-pond scum, etc. The patients need to be listened to, to have their feelings validated, and then to be refocused on the reality of their childhood and how it affected them. Because this is such a difficult, yet essential stage in therapy, we have devised some therapeutic stratagems to facilitate the patients' processes of reframing (their family-of-origin experience) and relearning (skills that were mis-taught or never taught in childhood).

The Picture. It is helpful for individuals raised in narcissistic families to have a realistic idea of who they were as children. One of their childhood coping mechanisms often was to think of themselves as somehow responsible for the problems in the family (as bad, defective, stupid, and so forth) in an attempt to gain control, believing "if I broke it, I can fix it." As adults, they still have a skewed idea of how responsible (or powerful) they were—how much control they had, and who they were as children. A technique that is helpful as a reality check is to ask the patient to obtain a picture of herself between the ages of three and seven, choose a special frame for it, and put it in a place where she will see it often. The picture makes the patient see herself as she really was; the special frame confers specialness and preciousness to the picture/child within it; and having to see the picture often forces the patient to deal more readily with facing the reality of the past.

This is always an interesting and enlightening exercise for the patient. At every phase, it presents her with opportunities for learning about the family-of-origin dynamic and about the child she was. The availability of pictures is often an issue: either there are not any, or the patient can not get one (she will!), or there are not any of her alone. The experience of shopping for a picture frame also presents a problem for many patients: she did not have time; they were too expensive; she could not find the right one; or she did not want to. We persist gently in encouraging the patient to procure a picture, acquire a suitable frame, and then choose a good location for its display. With such prodding, eventually she will be able to do this.

Looking at themselves as children is usually a shock for patients; adults are surprised at how small, how cute, and how lovable they seem. Sometimes the pictures are very sad, and sometimes they are happy. They all evoke memories and mirror some aspect of the reality of the patient's childhood. It is often extremely painful, however, for patients to look at the pictures, because they are a too-poignant reminder of the past and bring up too many feelings. This exercise can take weeks or even months to accomplish. What it does, eventually, accomplish is to drive home the reality: that they were children, not short adults; that they were small, powerless, and dependent. They controlled very little in their own life, let alone in anyone else's.

In later therapy, we often suggest that patients say positive messages to the child in the picture ("You are sweet," "You are so beautiful," "You deserved to be loved," "I love you," "You tried so hard to please," and so on). Since the adult patient may have spent a lot of time blaming her child self for the bad things that happened to her (especially in cases of overt abuse), this can be an important stage in the healing process. Again, it can take a long time. Especially in cases of sexual abuse, it is not uncommon for the adult to hate the child—to think of her as bad, dirty, nasty, weak, and the like. When this happens, it is often helpful for patients to go to parks or playgrounds where very young children are and to imagine that the abuse they themselves suffered was happening to one of the small children they are watching. Is that child bad? Does she deserve it? If the patient has children of her own, or any small child whom she loves as a part of her life, it is helpful for her to frame her own abuse in terms of that child: would my baby be responsible? Is she a bad little girl? Does she deserve whatever happened to me? The answer is invariably no.

Also later, we may have the patient bring little presents to the child in the picture: a flower is the most symbolic of acceptance and loving regard for most adults (male and female), but even a baseball card or a piece of candy—anything that denotes love to the patient—is positive.

When the adult can learn to accept and love the child in the picture, she is a long way toward being able to accept and love the adult version of that child. She is also more able to assess realistically conditions of responsibility and control—both past and present.

Compartmentalization. The concept of compartmentalization is important for patients, so that they can begin to discriminate between what they own (that is, can appropriately take responsibility for) and what someone else owns. One of the biggest problems for adults raised in narcissistic family systems is that they tend to take responsibility for things over which they have little or no control (such as things that happened when they were children with essentially no power), yet refuse to take responsibility for what is happening to them today (when they are adults, with a great deal of power over the decisions they make and the actions they perform).

Mark's Story.   Mark is a twenty-nine-year-old man who entered therapy to deal with depression. In the course of therapy, Mark remembered that he had been molested by his family's priest for a period of about five years, starting around seven years of age. Mark's devoutly Roman Catholic family had lived in poverty for years since his father had contracted cancer. His father was an invalid for that time, and he died when Mark was twelve. "Father Ted" was very kind to the family, and Mark's mother adored him. He helped the family in many ways and was especially solicitous to Mark, the oldest child and only boy. He took Mark to baseball games, car shows, the movies, and fishing, and gave the boy a whole range of positive experiences he would otherwise not have had. Father Ted was the family hero. It was, therefore, incredibly painful for Mark when the memories of his sexual molestation by Father Ted surfaced.

Mark went through many periods of saying to himself, "I made this all up; I'm sick; he never would have done this!" Of course he knew it had happened, but accepting the reality was as threatening for the adult Mark as the experience had been for the child Mark. Mark then defended against the painful reality by "adultamorphosing" his childhood self: "I could have stopped it if I'd wanted to; it was all my fault; I must have done something to make him believe it was what I wanted; I was a really bad/dirty boy." Mark was assuming the responsibility for his own abuse, investing his child self with power and control the child did not have.

Conversely, Mark was consistently abdicating his genuine adult control by making statements like "I can't deal with this; this will kill my mother; I'm not angry at anyone; even if it did happen, there's no point in talking about it now." He initially refused to get a picture, to keep a journal (see "Feeling Journal" in Chapter Five)—in other words, to assume responsibility for his recovery. Eventually

Mark saw that he could take responsibility for experiencing his anger in a positive way, rather than denying it in depression. He learned that he had a lot of control over his life *now* and that it was appropriate to take responsibility for it. At the same time he was finally able to see that he had *not* had control in childhood and therefore could not take on the responsibility for his own victimization. The use of the picture technique helped Mark to make this differentiation.

The Problem of Generalization. Adults from narcissistic families tend to generalize issues of responsibility and blame so that they end up with all-or-nothing stances. Depending on the day of the week, phase of the moon, or attitude of the maitre d', they decide that they are responsible for everything ("Oh, no! It's raining! Was it something I said?") or nothing ("So I told him if he didn't like my coming into work three hours late wearing jeans, he could take his job and shove it where the sun don't shine!")

The tendency to generalize is also demonstrated as a propensity to lump unrelated occurrences together, as if there were a cause-and-effect relationship. The following vignette illustrates this point:

Marie: I'm such a total loser. I bounced three checks, Johnnie failed his spelling test, and the water heater broke.
Therapist: I'm missing something here. I don't agree that you're a loser, although I can certainly understand why you might feel that way after bouncing three checks. I can't see the connection with Johnnie's test and the water heater, though.
Marie: I'm just a screwup. If I were a more competent person, these things wouldn't happen!
Therapist: You're saying that your son wouldn't have failed his spelling test and your water heater wouldn't have broken if you were more competent?
Marie: Right!

In order to assess issues of responsibility and control realistically, survivors need to be able to put their emotions about different events into separate compartments, to differentiate kinds of feelings, severity and immediacy of situations, depth of responsibility, and degree of power/control.

The Boxes. One of the tools that we have found useful with patients in teaching the skill of compartmentalization (as a deterrent to generalization) is "the boxes." In its most rudimentary form, it is used to teach the concept that differing realities can exist simultaneously; for instance, that:

- a father had an abysmal childhood, was forced to work sixty hours a week at a rotten job, married a woman who later abandoned him and their three children, and did the best he could to keep his family together, and that

- a child grew up afraid and insecure, sad and frightened by his father's coldness, feeling that there was no one to protect him because of his father's absence, always feeling stupid and worthless because he could not get his father to pay attention to him, and always feeling defective because he was just a baby when his mother chose to leave him.

In therapy, we would call the first item above "Box 1." In that box, we tell the patient, is your father's reality: long hours, poverty, fear, lack of parenting skills, no time, no help, feeling that he was doing the best he could. The patient can understand this and can recognize how tough things were for his dad. That box can be put aside, then, and we can look at "Box 2." Box 2, representing the second item above, contains the reality of the adult child's experience: trying to be invisible, feeling scared and inadequate, working so hard all the time with no praise, feeling alone, hoping that by achieving more and not causing trouble he could get some attention—and always failing.

The patient is helped to understand that both conditions, both boxes, existed. The fact that Dad tried hard does *not* mean that the boy was not damaged. Both boxes are real and exist on their own; one can be put away while the other is explored. This is the essence of compartmentalization.

In the more complex form of this technique, the patient is engaged in a game in which he designs imaginary boxes to hold different categories of feelings. He is asked to describe the box relative to a variety of parameters. The technique is valuable in terms of helping patients to recognize, label, and thus validate feelings, but also in terms of helping them to gain a sense of mastery and control.

It allows the patient, through visualization, to see that his situational feelings are finite: if you can put something in a box, then it has size, shape, and mass—that is, you can quantify it. *And what we can quantify, we can control.*

This game can get very complex as the patient "gets into" it and starts coming up with elaborate sizes, shapes, colors, and decorations. This form of the boxes technique requires the patient to describe the following:

1. Box contents ("Susie's Chores," "Visiting Hospitals," "My Job," "The Trip to Phil's Mother," "Vietnam," "Going to Church," "Fear," "Revenge," "Our Finances," "The Accident," "Cocaine," and so on)

2. Box Organization (all jammed in, neatly folded, in a ball, stacked, messy, carefully wrapped in layers of tissue, doused with grease and dirt, washed and ironed, and so on)

3. Box appearance (pink; black; cheap, tacky orange; covered with pink flowered chintz fabric; all squashed and battered; square; a hatbox; pale lavender with silver glitter glued on; huge; tiny and round; and so on)

4. Bow appearance (black, tied in a knot; big, puffy satin; thin, elegant silver-blue velvet tied flat; a clothesline; no bow, just nailed shut; and so on)

5. Where it goes (in the closet, buried in the back; on the dresser; in the sunshine on the back porch; under the winter boots; on top of an erupting volcano; and so on—"Send it to Hong Kong; by the time they figure out the mistake and send it back, I'll have figured out what to do with it!" and "Put it on the closet shelf under my husband's bowling bag, so if he tries to peek in it, the bowling ball will fall out and hit him on the head!" are two of our favorite patient responses)

(For a description of a therapy session using this technique, see Appendix B, "Therapy with the Blakes.")

When you are working with the concept of acceptance, therefore, the patient may have one box labeled "parents' situation" (or "Mom and Dad"), for instance, and another labeled "my feelings" (or "little Jimmy"). The patient can then put all the reasons for his parents' actions (and all their other attributes, like "no money," "Dad beat her," "baked cookies," "tried his best," and so on) into the first box. In the patient's box might be "felt unloved," "tried to be good," "fat," "always felt stupid," "feel inadequate," "don't know how to relate with people," and so forth.

The therapist is therefore able to underscore for the patient that these boxes are two distinct entities. They are different sizes, look different, and are stored in different places. They do not relate physically to each other; the contents do not get mixed up because they are both closed and tied. They are both real and exist simultaneously on their own merits. They are both valid. Regardless of the reasons for the contents of the parents' box, the reality is that the child's needs did not get met. It is those unmet childhood needs that make up the bulk of the adult patient's box.

Shedding of Denial. The first stage of acceptance might well be called "the shedding of denial." This stage does not imply either guilt or blame; it is simply an acceptance of reality. It may be the first time the patient has ever been encouraged to look at the reality of his or her upbringing. It is always painful. Farther down the line, of course, the patient may well assign blame and experience tremendous anger. But if blame is encouraged initially, then some patients will be too overwhelmed to continue, and they may drop out of therapy prematurely.

Stage Two: Mourning the Loss of the Fantasy

This stage is both the most painful and the most liberating for patients. On the one hand, the recognition that the "perfect" family can never be re-created (because it never existed in the first place) is an occasion for sorrow. It seems to remove for most patients the last vestiges of hope for a "real family." On the other hand, patients begin to see that as they stop wasting their emotional energy trying to re-create a situation that never was and to win approval they will never get, they now have enormous energy to expend on hopeful situations—on trying to create a fulfilling life on their own, and with people who may genuinely wish to meet their needs.

Adults raised in narcissistic homes cling to the fantasy that they can somehow manipulate or control their parent/family-of-origin system to get the recognition and approval they require (that is, to get their needs met.) They had this fantasy as children, and they maintain it as adults. The reality, though, is that they had little control over their parent system as children and have little control over it now.

One often encounters in these individuals the "hope springs eternal" phenomenon: the continual return to family-of-origin situations, with the knowledge that "this time," it will work out; (this Thanksgiving, we'll all get along; this Christmas, everyone will get everything they want, Mom won't get drunk, it will snow—I can make it happen). They believe they can re-create the perfect family they never had. But they could not "make it happen" then, and they cannot now.

Concentrating energy on that fantasy is destructive for several reasons:

1. It presupposes that the patient is somehow wrong, or defective; if she could just do better, be different, find the key, then she could get her needs met. In short, it blames the victim.

2. It keeps the patient involved with the family-of-origin system, which may preclude creating or adequately maintaining her own family or relationships of choice. It is a waste of time.

3. It keeps the patient fixed on a goal that she can never achieve: getting her needs met by her parent system. It is a set-up for failure.

4. It sets up a situation where opportunities for good interaction with the parent system—if they ever occur—will probably be missed because the constant underlying unrealistic expectations and resultant anger will make any kind of relaxed interaction impossible. It creates a pattern of missed opportunities.

Once the patient is able to mourn the loss of what might have been (but in reality, of course, could never be), she can then move on. She could not and cannot change her family of origin, but she does have the power and control to change herself and improve the quality of her life. Also, she may open up the possibility of developing a reality-based relationship with her family of origin once she stops trying to manipulate, control, and gain approval. In other words, she may decide to melt down the bedpan.

Stage Three: Recognition

The third stage of acceptance involves recognizing those effects of being raised in a narcissistic family that are evidenced in the individual's life now. This means being able to look at specific personality traits and saying, "Aha! I see where that came from." For instance, a patient might say, "I can never be assertive, I can never tell people how I feel. Now I understand that I can never tell people because I don't *know* how I feel. I don't know how I feel because when I was a child, no one ever asked me how I felt. In fact, in order to survive in my family of origin, I had to bury my feelings. Not only were they unimportant, but they were potentially dangerous. I was not allowed to have feelings." This stage is a recognition of present traits as they reflect past experience.

An important therapeutic consideration is that the patient needs to be told that although those traits developed in childhood may be dysfunctional now (in adulthood), they were valuable at the time. Those traits and skills allowed the child to continue to function within his narcissistic family; they need to be *valued* by the therapist as sensible coping mechanisms in a difficult situation. Now, of course, the situation has changed (he is an adult; he has power and control), and his coping mechanisms may need to change as well. It is vital in the formation of a positive self-image, however, for the patient to be encouraged to have respect for the child he was, and for that child's ability to survive. He is, after all, essentially a bigger, older version of that child: he deserved respect then, and he deserves it now.

Most children of narcissistic families have a difficult time dealing with any kind of criticism, overt or implied. They take a rejection of anything they do, think, say, or feel as a rejection of themselves. Their self-image is too amorphous, and therefore too vulnerable, to deal with negative feedback. The therapeutic considerations again have to deal with validating and respecting the child's survival mechanisms, as well as validation of the adult's need to change some of them. Many of these individuals become "people pleasers" in an attempt to head off negative feedback before it can happen. For them, everyone out there becomes a mirror of their own self-worth ("if no one gets mad at me, I'm okay"; "if anyone—from the boss to a neighborhood child—gets mad at me, criticizes me, or looks at me funny, then I'm bad, stupid, worthless"; and so on). They believe that they are as others react to them.

Going Back to the Well.   In the recognition stage, survivors also experience a phenomenon that we call "going back to the well." This simply means that they decide to apply the insights and strengths they have gained from therapy to enable their successful return to dysfunctional situations. They believe that they are now ready to reenter those situations (a narcissistic family of origin, an alcoholic marriage, or an abusive relationship) and effect a different outcome. Now that they have all this knowledge, they think that they are strong enough to go back and make it come out better—because *this time* they will not get sucked in. This behavior tends to resurface most strongly around such annual occasions as birthdays, Thanksgiving, Christmas, or wedding anniversaries. This desire to use newly gained skills to enable old maladaptive behaviors can drive therapists up the proverbial wall.

We tell patients a story that uses the "going back to the well" metaphor to help them understand what they are doing:

> Let's say that there is a well in your backyard. It's very quaint looking: round, made of old stones, with a little roof on top, and a bucket that you can lower to draw up cool, sweet water. You have many fond childhood memories of going out to the well, maybe with a grandparent or sibling or parent, and they would help you to pull the bucket up. You felt important and proud that you could get the water. Then one day you discovered that the well had been poisoned. When you drank the water, it made you sick. You were very sad that you could never go to the well and get that good water again. You thought and thought about it, and you came up with an idea: I'll go back to the well, but I'll use a *New Bucket*! So you buy a bucket, get the water, drink it—and get sick. The next day you decide to try to get the water in your favorite mug, the one with the cows on it, you drink it, and you get sick. So you decide to try the water out of a plastic glass, through a straw—you still get sick. You try to drink the water standing on your head . . .

The patients get the point. When you go back into dysfunctional, hurtful situations with the expectation that you can "make it better," you are setting yourself up for failure and pain.

Recognition of these behavior patterns, which are shared by many people raised in narcissistic families, is a crucial part of recovery. This is the basis for reforming the molten gold.

Stage Four: Evaluation

Evaluation involves the patients' assessment of her current situation: looking at the personality traits that she now "owns" and deciding which ones she may wish to keep, and which ones are now no longer functional and need to be changed.

In this stage, patients often regress to a lot of self-blame; they will make comments like, "my parents really weren't that bad," and "I feel guilty coming in here and bad-mouthing my family every week; it's not really fair, you know, because you're only hearing my side of the story." We usually respond with something like, "This isn't a court of law; we're not here to decide the 'Truth,' we're here to talk about your feelings and perceptions. If your parents want to talk about their feelings and perceptions, they can go out and get their own therapist."

Because patients again at this stage tend to "get stuck" in all the ways they have "screwed up" their lives, all the bad choices they have made, all the things they did not say and should have (and vice versa), all the people they have let walk all over them, and so forth, it is very important that the therapist constantly give the patient positive reinforcement. One of the ways of doing this without appearing to give a compliment merely for the sake of doing so ("blowing sunshine up my ass," as one patient so elegantly referred to it) is to reflect the following:

- the patient was operating with limited information at the time, and he made his decisions based on that limited information,
- the patient's coping mechanisms may not be working for him now, but they kept him going—maybe even kept him alive—as a child. It was good that he developed them, not bad; he may in adulthood, however, wish to develop new ones.

At this time, the patient is developing a blueprint for the work of art he will make with his gold.

Stage Five: Responsibility for Change

The fifth stage of acceptance, then, is to work on changing those personality traits that may have been functional in childhood and indeed may have facilitated survival, but that are now dysfunctional in adult life and are definitely getting in the individual's way. It is at this stage that the therapist is especially valuable to the patient. The therapist can present healthy options and possibilities to the patient that have not been part of the latter's milieu.

Janine's Story.   Janine entered therapy with complaints of chronic anxiety and a pervasive exhaustion. She indeed looked exhausted, and her affect was both anxious and depressed. She had been to a number of physicians, none of whom were able to identify the source of the problem. She had been prescribed sleeping pills, antidepressants, tranquilizers, and vitamins, none of which had been of more than temporary help in alleviating her exhaustion and anxiety.

The product of a narcissistic family with a workaholic, judgmental father and a religiously committed, long-suffering, and passive mother, Janine had been raised in the Bible Belt to believe that her only purpose on earth was to serve others. She missed school if help was needed around the house or farm; she never dated or participated in after-school events, because that would encourage selfishness. No one questioned that it was only Janine who had these sacrifices; her brothers were never asked to miss school, and they participated freely in athletics and other after-school activities. Janine, however, was told that her body was a "vessel for sin," and that the only hope she had for redemption would come from selfless service to others. Assertiveness or boundaries were not words that came trippingly to the tongue for Janine; they were not integrated with her worldview in any way. As a matter of fact, as she confessed after two years of therapy, she would never have entered therapy if she had known that she would be encouraged to become more assertive. She came to therapy to figure out why she was so weak, and she left realizing that she had strengths she had never been allowed to explore.

During the course of therapy, Janine was able to identify that she had few if any boundaries. She was married, with four children, and she was literally a slave to all of them. Further, she felt unable to say no to virtually anyone who asked anything of her—no matter how inappropriate or

bizarre the request might be. At various times she had taken
care of neighbors' pets (in spite of being allergic to animal
hair), baby-sat other people's children at all hours of the day
or night, provided transportation back and forth to Boston
(a two-hour trip each way) for a neighbor she barely knew
(and who in fact had been rude and insulting to her), stayed
up all night typing a term paper for her teenage daughter
when she herself had pneumonia, and on and on. The
woman did not know that refusal was an option. In her family of origin she was physically and verbally abused for
refusal, or even for lack of enthusiasm. Saying no was quite
simply not a choice that had been available to her.

Janine's therapist was able to introduce the concept that
there was a middle ground between being totally inaccessible
(her parent model) and totally accessible (her reactive parenting mode), and that it was appropriate for her to evaluate
requests and demands on the basis of her available time,
energy, and interest. It was the beginning of major changes
in Janine's life. "No" was now an option. There were, of
course, many other issues that Janine dealt with in the
course of therapy, but the idea that refusal was a valid option
was the beginning of her recovery—the transformation of
her molten gold into something of beauty.

Blame and Confrontation

As we have mentioned before, patients, especially those who are
religiously committed, often report having tried therapy before but
being unable to continue because it was held out to them that they
must "hate" or "reject" or "confront" their parent (or whomever the
dysfunctional caretaker was). The concepts of blame and confrontation are not essential to the implementation of this model; they are
individual issues that each patient/therapist dyad must deal with on
a case-by-case basis. In working for years within this model, we have
noted that patients feel more able to get in touch with their anger in
the absence of blaming statements by the therapist. Because they
have no need to defend the parent system, they are more able to
look at it realistically.

When the Narcissistic Family was Traumatically Abusive: The Issue of Confrontation

The wish to confront a perpetrator/victimizer, especially in cases of sexual abuse and assaultive physical abuse, is often extremely strong in the early stages of therapy. We have found in our work with survivors of childhood sexual abuse, that very soon after memories start to surface, the survivor's impulse—especially if the survivor is male—is to run right out and confront the victimizer, with the intent of "making [him or her] *pay* for what [he or she] did to me."

Confrontation in these early stages does not work. The patient is doing it for the wrong reasons and gets hurt in the process. In our group practice, which has seen hundreds of survivors, confrontations that were thought by the therapist to be premature but were engaged in against his or her advice have been damaging. The confrontation itself then becomes a focus of therapy for weeks, and the patient's progress is impaired.

Confrontation is necessary and desirable for many, but not all patients. Often by the time of therapy the perpetrator is dead or has moved away. A symbolic gesture is used in those cases: role-play confrontation in the therapist's office, a letter written and burned, a visit to the cemetery to deliver a letter or to tell the dead person how the survivor feels. Where possible, a direct one-on-one confrontation, or a meeting between the survivor and perpetrator in the therapist's office, is often an important step in the healing process. But this is only true when the patient is doing it for the right reason.

The "right reason" has to with the patient's expectations for the confrontation. If he wants revenge, to get an apology, to cause physical harm, to get the perpetrator to admit that he or she did it, to "watch her squirm," or to "clear the air so we can start all over," the intervention will fail. In fact, *if the patient wants anything at all from the perpetrator, the confrontation is a set-up for failure.* He will walk out feeling worse than when he went in, because all he will have done will be to reenact an old scenario. He will be trying to impact the parent/perpetrator system—to change, control, manipulate, or affect it—and he can not. He does not have that power or control. Of course he can "go public" with it, but that is a double-edged sword, too, and needs careful consideration with the therapist.

The right reason for confrontation is to enable the survivor to tell the perpetrator what happened and how the survivor feels about it;

how what the perpetrator did to him has affected his life, his feelings about himself and the world; how much pain the perpetrator has caused him; and how he now feels about the perpetrator. It is a purely selfish act. It is not to change the perpetrator, or to make him admit what he did. It is not about the perpetrator; it is about the survivor. For once, the survivor will have an opportunity to validate his childhood experience and talk about his feelings. The perpetrator's reaction is irrelevant. When the patient can write the letter, or set up the meeting, with no expectations of the perpetrator, the confrontation will be successful. The patient will have accomplished his goal.

It is helpful for the therapist to anticipate that the wish to confront will strike prematurely, and to be ready to deal with it. In early sessions, when the patient is just starting to have memories or flashbacks, we introduce the possibility of confrontation as an option, something the patient may or may not want to do, at some time in the (distant) future. When the strong urge comes on to confront prematurely, we suggest that the patient put it off "until next week. Let's not do it this week—let's give it a week and think about it." Or we say, "Why don't you bring the letter in before you mail it? We can go over it together and make sure that it says what you really want it to say." We are up-front about telling the patient that it is premature, and why we believe that to be the case. But we also do it in a gentle way, leaving the door open to "next week" or "bringing the letter in" so that the patient does not feel cut off or shut down. Then, if the patient goes ahead and confronts against our advice, they will feel less shameful about disclosing it to us, because the door was left open—even if it was just a crack.

Forgiveness

On the other side of the coin, forgiveness is not an essential part of this model either. When confronted with the issue of forgiving the perpetrator(s), our belief is that the issue is more in the spiritual domain than in the psychological. Although the issue of forgiveness has been dealt with at length by Scott Peck, Bass and Davis, and others, we do not pursue it.[2] In our experience, the self-imposed pressure to forgive the perpetrator often gets in the way of genuine recovery, as it can act to shut off the patient's necessary expression of anger and self-validation of feelings. When patients ask about the subject, we usually respond by telling them that in our experience, forgiveness is a feeling or condition of being more than an act. As such, it can not be legislated or decided upon; if it happens, it happens on its own. Within this model, forgiveness is no more necessary than blame. The patient is asked for a reflection of reality, not a judgment call.

Conclusion

Acceptance of the realities of growing up in a narcissistic family is more than half the battle toward recovery. Again, a particularly helpful aspect of this model is that, as we underscored earlier, it does not imply blame or judgment, confrontation, or forgiveness. It implies recognition of how we learned what we learned, and how we can relearn it to make life more satisfying. It removes responsibility for dysfunction from the patient as a child, but places responsibility for recovery on him or her as an adult. Again, he or she has been molded by his past experiences, but needs to no longer be defined by them.

5
Feelings and Communication

In the Narcissus myth, Echo was unable to advocate for herself; she was unable to express her feelings, and she died. This is a vivid metaphor for the need to be in touch with our feelings, and the need to find ways to express them assertively and—we hope—be successful in getting our needs met.

Viktor Frankel, two thousand years after Ovid, illustrates the concept of the essential need to express our feelings in his story of a fellow concentration camp survivor. The conditions of their lives in the camp caused severe swelling in the feet, making it impossible for the prisoners to put their boots on before going out to the work details. Only one prisoner was able to pull his boots on. When Frankel asked him how he had managed to rid himself of the edema, he replied, "I have wept it out of me." As Frankel explains, "There was no need to be ashamed of tears, for tears bore witness that a man had the greatest courage, the courage to suffer."[1]

For adults from narcissistic families, the concept of recognizing and validating one's own feelings is often far removed from their family-of-origin experience. The skill of appropriate communication of feelings, then, becomes a monumental task: how can I verbally communicate that which I cannot internally acknowledge? If one has not been taught that one has the right to feel, then one has certainly not been taught how to communicate feelings in a direct and assertive manner.

Teaching patients how to be appropriately assertive is often the therapist's biggest challenge when working with survivors of narcissistic families. Teaching and learning this multilevel skill—allowing oneself to experience feelings by recognizing, labeling, self-validating, and appropriately expressing them, culminating in a clear statement of expectations—is an enormously complex task. It cuts to the very heart of the survivor's condition: if I don't know who I am, how can I explain me to you?

The model we use for teaching effective communication skills is called "I feel . . . I want."[2] Essentially, it calls for the verbal expression of one's feelings, followed by a clear expression of what one wants:

> Tommy, I feel angry and hurt that you didn't pick up the family room after you promised that you would. I would like you to do it now.

"I feel . . . I want" is obvious and simple, but most people do not know how to do it. It avoids game playing, misunderstandings, explosive scenes, inaccurate mind reading, and all manner of evil things. It is the best model for clear, respectful communication that we have encountered.

For individuals raised in narcissistic families, assertiveness is a major problem. There are two parts to assertiveness: knowing how one feels, and being able to express that in a clear, nonaggressive manner. As indicated in Chapter Two, both knowledge of feelings and expression of them are difficult tasks for survivors.

In our practice, we much prefer the term *respectful adult communication* to *assertiveness*. Although *assertiveness* is a perfectly respectable and functional word, it has a negative connotation for many patients. It is also less descriptive. Essentially, patients need to learn to respect themselves and others, to learn to relate as fully functioning adults, and to communicate effectively so that the message sent is indeed the message received. We have, therefore, divided this chapter into two parts (on identifying and expressing feelings, respectively) and have set forth a number of therapeutic techniques for use in the teaching of these important skills.

Identifying Feelings

Many patients are uncomfortable even with the the word *feelings*. As one patient commented, "I don't go for all that huggy-touchy crunchy-granola stuff!" It is therefore necessary to help patients develop some degree of comfort in the discussion of feelings, so that they can recognize (1) what feelings are, and (2) that they experience them. To that end, we have described a number of techniques used in our practice.

Listing Feelings

It is often interesting and helpful to spend time with the patient simply listing feelings. Many cannot, without prompting, come up with even one feeling! Or they may be able to come up with "upset," "sad," "happy," "good," or "bad," and that is all. Patients are usually astonished by the number of feelings that can be generated in a list with their therapist.

These individuals will say things like "I don't have feelings," or "It hurts too much to feel." They have no concept of the importance or function of feelings. Within the framework of the narcissistic family model, we teach survivors that feelings:

- are the truest expression of who we are;
- exist on their own;
- cannot be legislated (as in, "you should love your brother");
- are not right or wrong, or good or bad—they just are;
- are instinctual and often protective;
- motivate us to necessary action (for example, "I feel afraid, therefore I will call the police");
- need to be tuned in to and honored; because they
- will come out—even if we ignore, deny, or stuff them—in physical symptoms, explosive anger, or depression (anger's "other face").

Feelings are especially valuable as motivators to action, as in Bradshaw's use of the concept of "E-motion."[3] Therefore, when we deny our emotions or feelings, we may not take necessary and appropriate actions. As therapists know, inaction all too often leads to depression.

There are a number of techniques that are helpful in teaching adults from narcissistic homes how to recognize and label their feelings. Three that we frequently use (the body language test, feeling stories, and video projection) are detailed below. We also recommend that patients maintain "feeling journals" in which they identify and label feelings they experience, including physical sensations.

The Body Language Test

Most people experience strong feelings as one or more physical sensations: for instance, as a constriction in the throat, or the sense that one's stomach or heart is lodged at the base there; as a tightening in the neck and shoulder muscles; or as an instant headache. Some individuals experience almost instantaneous symptoms of stomachache or diarrhea in times of emotional distress. Ask the patient where she feels emotion (or upset) in her body; most likely, she will have no trouble telling you.

The first step, then, is to have the patient tune in to her symptom—really notice and experience it, and get praise from the therapist for just allowing herself to experience the feeling physically.

> **Mary's Story.** Mary is a thirty-year-old woman whose narcissistic family of origin was composed of a quiet, nonassertive father, an intrusive and emotionally abusive mother, and two sisters. Mary's mother would call Mary several times a week and "dump" on her, regaling her with stories of all the bad things her sisters were doing; she would always attempt to draw Mary into complex and upsetting family scenarios. Mary had been seeing a chiropractor for over a year for neck tightness and pain. She had labeled the pain as an offshoot of a minor automobile accident, assuming that she experienced pain when she inadvertently stressed her back or neck by lifting or twisting wrong. Referred by her chiropractor for therapy, she had come to the conclusion that the pain might be more an expression of psychological distress than of physical injury.
>
> During the course of therapy, Mary started keeping a feeling journal in which she tracked her neck pain and the

events, thoughts, and feelings she had experienced during the course of the day. She was also taught Benson's "relaxation response," which she learned to employ when she became aware of her neck pain.[4] By keeping the journal, Mary was able to link her physical symptoms to specific events and thoughts—the triggers for the feelings—and to *label* the feelings that were being expressed in her neck as pain.

Therapist: Mary, this week when you felt the neck tightness, were you able to link it to something that happened, or to something you were thinking about?

Mary: It's funny, but I always noticed that I seem to feel more pain on weekends, but I never knew why. In my journal, it tells why! I get it after my mother calls [on the telephone]. She calls a lot on the weekends, because my dad works then. This time, when I hung up I realized that I had that pain. And I hadn't done anything—physical, I mean—to hurt myself.

Therapist: So your mother is a pain in the neck?

Mary: (*laughing*) I guess so.

Therapist: Mary, what were you feeling during that conversation?

Mary: I was wishing that she wouldn't call me all the time and dump on me.

Therapist: Okay, but that's what you were *thinking*. I want to know how you were feeling. If the word *that* is in there, you are describing a thought, not a feeling. What did you feel?

Mary: I felt that—no. I felt angry. Really angry. Furious.

At this point the therapist was able to praise Mary for the work she was doing, and to underscore the steps that she was taking to change her life for the better. Patients often have a difficult time in recognizing their successes and will frequently acknowledge them in terms that actually reflect deficit or failure ("Yeah, maybe I did it this time, but I *should* have been doing it all along!") It is important that the therapist reframe the experience as a deficit of *training* rather than of intelligence, moral fiber, or whatever: the patient did not have the skills (training, options, worldview) then, but she is learning them now.

A significant part of therapy in this model is that the therapist is action oriented, rather than primarily reflective or supportive. It is important that the therapist verbally reward the patient for appropriate behavior by making laudatory statements and reframing— not in the sense of cheerleading for the patient, but rather to reflect the reality of the work she is doing. This way, the patient will know when she has done a "good thing." She probably did not get this kind of feedback during childhood, so she needs and appreciates it now.

The final step is to enable the patient to express the feeling and to take some action to attend to it.

> After considerable discussion, Mary decided to express her feelings to her mother and set some boundaries on the relationship. "Using 'I feel . . . I want', I'm going to tell her that I feel very angry when she calls me up and complains about my sisters and brothers, and that I don't want her to do it anymore."
>
> After a few tentative efforts, Mary was able to express her feelings to her mother, and she in fact terminated a number of conversations when her mother "broke the rule." After a period during which her mother refused to speak to Mary at all (giving her "the silent treatment"), her mother changed her telephone behavior. She began to call Mary less frequently, to Mary's relief, and the conversations were briefer, with more acceptable discussion topics. Her mother then started to call one of Mary's sisters and dump on her instead. As Mary said, "Now it's my sister's problem; she's just going to have to learn to deal with it!"
>
> As Mary learned, people continue to use certain interactive techniques because they work; the tactics get them what they want. When those techniques no longer work, people stop using them. As long as Mary was willing to listen to her mother (that is, meet her mother's needs), her mother continued to dump on her. When that no longer worked—when Mary refused to listen (started to respect herself) and was able to communicate that in an adult, clear manner—her mother stopped dumping on her. Mary thus was able to affect a modification of her mother's behavior, at least in relation to her.
>
> Further, Mary learned that her body was a valuable tool for indicating to her when she was experiencing a feeling

that required attention. Instead of regarding her neck pain as an enemy, Mary realized that it was a protective warning of high stress. By learning to attend to her body language and to act on it, she was under less stress and subsequently experienced markedly diminished neck pain.

Feeling Stories

It is often difficult for survivors to attribute feelings to themselves, especially if experiencing feelings was painful, not productive, or punished in the past. A time-honored method of eliciting feelings for diagnostic purposes has been through use of projective techniques (Thematic Apperception Test, Rorschach tests, and the like).[5] Using this method from a therapeutic perspective (rather than a diagnostic one), we have found that asking patients to imagine what *other* people might feel in a given situation is far less threatening for them and is, further, an excellent technique for recognizing and labeling feelings.

Feeling stories are short vignettes that the therapist can improvise spontaneously in the office. Not only can these stories be helpful in getting patients to identify and label feelings, they often act as a "memory spur" (something that aids in or triggers the retrieval/recollection of buried memories). In therapy, the practitioner will tell the feeling story and then have the patient decide how the character or characters in the story might be feeling:

> A little girl is playing with a cat in the yard. She goes inside for a drink of water, and the cat runs into the road and is struck by a car. How does the little girl feel?
>
> A boy is playing with some kids when they start to pick on a smaller boy. He doesn't do anything; he just watches. Pretty soon the smaller boy runs away, crying. How does the first boy feel?
>
> A boy is always getting beaten up by his father. One day, the father comes in very angry because the boy's skateboard was in the driveway and the father tripped over it. The boy's sister knows that the boy will be beaten again, so she lies to the father and says that *she* left the skateboard outside. The father beats her instead of the brother. How does she feel?

When the brother finds out about it (from another sibling), how does he feel?

A girl has a mother who plays with her and reads to her and cuddles her a lot. But when the girl's father is scary and yells bad things at the girl, the mother pretends not to notice or goes into another room. How does the girl feel?

A boy wins a poetry contest and is asked to read his poem to his class. How does he feel?

A girl's mother frequently breaks her promises to her, then afterward buys the girl a nice present. How does the girl feel?

A girl is outside playing with her friends when it starts to get dark. The friends all begin to leave. The girl asks them to stay out and play with her. They tell her that their parents told them to come home when the street lights come on. She says that her parents don't have any rules about when she has to come home. How does she feel?

Although the appropriate feelings may seem obvious, it is fascinating to experience the ease/difficulty with which patients answer the "feeling" questions. It is also diagnostically valuable to note the differing kinds of responses elicited based on individual patients' experiences. For instance, one patient responded to the first story (about the cat being hit by the car) by saying, "She felt happy. It was her sister's cat, and the girl always hated it. She wanted a dog. Her mother said they could only have one pet, and her older sister got to choose. She *always* got to choose. Now, since the cat is dead, the girl can get a dog!" Notice as well the difference in the responses below of two female patients to the story of the children playing when the street lights came on.

(**Chris** is a well-educated professional woman in her mid-thirties who is both anxious and depressed. She was raised by an intrusive, extremely critical father who had unrealistically high expectations for her, and a mother who was so passive that the possibility of chronic low-level depression is raised.) "It's hard for me to imagine no rules! Wow!" (Some embarrassed laughter.) "The girl is lucky. She feels . . . proud. Her parents trust her to use her own judgment. Her parents love her a lot."

(**Laura** is a highly intelligent, undereducated mother of three young children. She is a recovering alcoholic who was abused by her mother—who then abandoned the family when Laura was nine years old—neglected by her compulsive gambler father, and molested by her stepbrother.) "She feels so ashamed. All those other kids have people who care about them—who want them home—who care enough to make rules. She would *kill* to have somebody care. Nobody cares if she comes home or not; they don't even notice.

Feelings that are too painful for the patient to express directly often get revealed during these story sessions. Many children from narcissistic families have such deeply buried memories that it takes a story about *another* child to release them. Most therapists have had the experience of receiving calls from patients who have had a flood of memories triggered by a television program or newspaper article. Feeling stories work in much the same way, but more efficiently. The therapist can often make educated guesses about the kinds of experiences the patient may have had that are being suppressed, and he or she can tailor the feeling stories accordingly.

For instance, the story of the boy who won the poetry contest was used with a young man who had been raised by an extremely macho father. The therapist suspected that the young man (who was clearly not homosexual) harbored fantasies and fears of being homosexual, which he found too frightening to acknowledge and discuss. When the feeling story was told to him, the dam burst. He was able to relate incident after incident of childhood experiences in which he attempted to form close friendships with other boys, only to have his father do or say something to ruin it. The boy was left always feeling bad and guilty—never knowing what he had done wrong, but knowing that there was something wrong with wanting close relationships with other males. In adolescence, this knowledge translated into the feeling that his father *knew* that way down deep inside, the boy was gay. Therefore, he always had to guard against that, since (of course) his father had special knowledge and insight. While his fears of homosexuality may well have come out in the course of therapy, the feeling story permitted the patient to spend his therapy time dealing directly with his feelings of fear, guilt, and shame, rather than losing weeks or months agonizing over how, when, and whether to disclose.

Video Projection

With this technique, patients are able to retell emotionally charged incidents in their past while maintaining a degree of detachment. The patient is asked to imagine a large television (or movie) screen; playing on it is the incident they find too painful to talk about. They then describe it in the third person. We use this technique extensively in combination with hypnosis for abreactive work with survivors of sexual abuse and other forms of posttraumatic stress disorder.

> **Margo's Story.**   Margo is a thirty-five-year-old real estate broker who owns her own business. She has been increasingly troubled by anxiety during the day and interrupted sleep at night. During the first few sessions of therapy, she has maintained that her family of origin—two successful, professional people—was idyllic. She has been exploring her sleep patterns in childhood with her therapist, who has asked her to make a movie of herself as a child, sleeping. She has already described the bedroom and the bed.

Margo: There is a girl. She's about nine or ten. She's in her bed, sleeping. Then—there's a strong light. The hall door was opened. The hall light is shining in.

Therapist: How does the girl feel?

Margo: She's sleepy. She wants to sleep. She's . . . sad.

Therapist: Why sad?

Margo: She knows she won't sleep well now. That makes her sad.

Therapist: What's happening now?

Margo: She's sad (*crying as she speaks*) for her little brother. It's her little brother at the door. Now he's closed it. He's crying; she can hear him sniffling. He's coming to the bed. She moves over to let him in. He cries, and she cuddles him. He goes to sleep. She's awake.

Therapist: How does she feel?

Margo: Sad. She's sad for her little brother . . . that he still cares. She doesn't. She's sad that she won't sleep any more.

Therapist: What's happening now?

Margo: She's looking at her little brother, watching him sleep. He looks so sweet. He's only five. He didn't close the hall door all the way, so there's some light falling on him (*starts to cry again*). She puts her arms around him and holds him.

Therapist: What is she feeling, Margo?

Margo: Sad.

Therapist: Is that all?

Margo: Sad . . . and mad. Angry. Full of rage. She hates those bastards. They upset him so much. They don't deserve a sweet little boy like Teddy. I hate them. He loves them, so he gets hurt. He needs to learn. To stop caring. (*Crying hard and rocking herself in her chair*) I hurt for him . . . and for me. I did care, but they f——ed it up. I had to take care of Teddy, but I was only a child. I couldn't do it right. He needed parents. . . . I needed parents. There was no one there to take care of us. No one.

As Margo was finally able to put the pieces together, the family's life was built around bolstering the mother's self-esteem and making her feel confident while not making too many demands on her. The nighttime problems would arise when Margo's parents, who had a very active social life, would come home from a party. The mother would start a fight with the father for paying too much attention to another woman, or for something he had or had not said or done in the course of the evening. The mother would always slam doors, which awakened Teddy. Then the fighting would escalate, the father would threaten to leave, and the mother would cry and beg him to forgive her. Teddy, whose room was next to the parents' bedroom, would become fearful and go into his sister's room in another wing of the house. Margo would feel intensely protective of her little brother (whom she adored), angry at her parents, and afraid for herself.

The use of video projection puts distance between the patient and the experience. It provides a margin of emotional safety, so that the patient does not "shut down" and block important memories.

Expressing Feelings

"I Feel . . . I Want"

Once individuals are able to (1) recognize that they have feelings and (2) label their feelings, they are then able to learn to express their feelings appropriately—the "I feel" part. When they are then able to accept (3) that they have a right to experience those feelings and (4) that their feelings are important, it becomes easier for them to verbalize their expectations to other people—the "I want" part. And as they quickly experience, once they are able to express the "I feel," it is often unnecessary to spell out the "I want." Much of the time, the most important thing is to be able to have feelings heard.

There are skills to be learned in the expression of feelings, however.[6] There is a list of "bad things" that people often say when they are experiencing strong emotions and having difficulty in expressing them (see list in Appendix B). While these behaviors (name calling, "you" references, "always/never" statements, gunnysacking, making historical references, and comparing the other with his or her parent, among others) work well to

- escalate emotions,
- hurt feelings,
- vent spleens,
- induce guilt and shame,
- produce defensiveness,
- encourage counterattacks, and
- preclude the possibility of problem solving.

They do not work well to communicate feelings and preferences in a way that they can be *heard* by the other person. Individuals who are talked to by someone using any of the negative techniques listed above do not feel valued or respected; they feel attacked. Humans don't listen well when they are being attacked, because they are preparing a defensive counterattack. This is not a good recipe for helpful, problem-solving-oriented communication. For instance, individuals will respond quite differently to "You always interrupt me! You're so inconsiderate!" than to "I feel hurt and angry when you interrupt me; I feel like my opinion doesn't matter. I feel stupid."

Conversely, humans do listen to statements describing feelings. Those statements are interesting, descriptive, and nonthreatening—they describe the speaker, not the listener. They are respectful of both parties, and they stand an excellent chance of being heard. There is no defense to prepare, because there is no attack to defend against. "I feel . . . I want" is respectful adult communication (RAC) at its best.

Caroline Revisited.   We often refer to Caroline (mentioned in Chapter Two, whose mother told her, "If you have to ask for it, it loses its value") when working with a patient on the concept of respectful adult communication, as her learning experience with "I feel . . . I want" hits home with most survivors.

> Caroline was hurt and angry that her husband continually forgot her birthday. Birthdays had not been a big deal in his family of origin, but they had been in Caroline's, and she had loved the attention and the presents and the feeling of being really special for one day. So she would get nervous as the "big day" approached—would he remember? The closer it got the more anxious she got, then angry ("Screw him if he can't remember!") and ultimately depressed (Screw me! It's no big deal; he shows me he loves me in other ways. I'm not a child any more.) Caroline couldn't remind him about her birthday because of her belief that asking for something made it lose its value. So, every year for the first three years of their marriage, she kept replaying that old mental tape and having a miserable birthday. And every year, there would be the postbirthday fight, tears, and misery, wherein her husband would explain all over again about birthdays in his family of origin and beg Caroline to remind him of her birthday; if she would tell him what she would like him to do, he would be overjoyed to do it.
>
> But Caroline just could not do it. The joys of martyrdom

were too deeply a part of her worldview. Caroline had commenced therapy a few weeks before her third birthday was celebrated in the marriage. The many options available to her for dealing with the celebration of her birthday—including the replaying of the old, familiar tape with the hope that somehow, this time, things would turn out differently—were discussed. (See "Going Back to the Well" in Chapter Four.) That was the option she chose, however, with the predictable result.

By the next birthday, Caroline was an expert in RAC. This is what she did:

1. three months before her birthday, she put a big sign up on the refrigerator door saying, "Caroline's Birthday is Coming!"
2. two months before, she replaced that sign with one saying, "Caroline's Birthday—Just 8 More Weeks!"
3. six weeks before, an updated sign was put on the refrigerator, and little pink sticky-notes started appearing throughout the house, with messages like "Caroline *loves* yellow roses!" and "Caroline's favorite restaurant is . . .," "Caroline *adores* Chanel #5," "Caroline wants a chocolate mousse birthday cake with candles!" and so forth.

It became a game. Caroline started having fun, and her husband was delighted. He very much wanted to please her, and now she was showing him exactly how to do it. Needless to say, she had a wonderful birthday! Caroline had turned a lose-lose situation into a win-win situation by using RAC— and very creatively, too.

Conclusion

The concept of respectful adult communication (RAC) seems so simple, yet it is based on a complex of attitudes and skills, the absence of any one of which makes RAC impossible. The therapist must be able to help the patient rediscover his feelings, learn how to recognize and label them, and then develop a level of both comfort and skill in communicating those feelings to others.

6
Setting Boundaries

The ability to set personal boundaries has long been recognized as an essential component of healthy functioning.[1] Boundaries have to do with ego differentiation—the old "yours, mine, and ours" concept. What is it that appropriately belongs to you, or to me, and what is it that we share? A person with good ego boundaries can make judgments about his or her appropriate accessibility to others (physically, emotionally, and mentally). He or she can say yes or no to all manner of things with relative comfort in the appropriateness of his or her judgments. (See Janine's story in Chapter Four.)

Ben's Story.　When one feels comfort with boundary setting, he does not have to agonize over minor decisions, as Ben did when he was asked to be on the school board: "I don't really have time to be on the school board; I can't do it. No. But—is that selfish? Other people do these things, I should be able to do it—for the kids. Okay. Yes. But—the kids will suffer if I'm out another night during the week. No. But—maybe that's just a cop-out because I'm tired a lot, or I'm afraid if I get on the board they'll figure out that I'm a dummy. So it's just my insecurity talking. Yes. I'll do it. But . . . I don't know what I should do! *You* tell me what to do!"

Ben (who was introduced in Chapter Two), did not have a clue about how to set personal boundaries. A harried divorced father of two school-age children, Ben was the product of a narcissistic family with a cold, judgmental, emotionally abusive mother and a detached, angry, physically abusive father whose expectations for Ben were cruelly high. Even when Ben met the expectations (which was often, as he was a brilliant scholar and gifted athlete), he never got praise, only a critique of how he could have performed better. Ben's entire childhood and adolescence was an elaborate attempt to hit the moving target of parental approval. He never could. By the time Ben was married (to a cold, disapproving woman with impossibly high expectations), he personified Kellogg's "human doing."[2] He was an achievement machine, with feelings buried so deeply that he was unable to identify what a feeling was. It was only after a sudden and unexpected (on his part) divorce plummeted him into a frightening and suicidal depression that Ben sought help.

To Ben, the divorce was the ultimate expression of his total inability to win approval, and the utter hopelessness of his life. From his perspective, he had done everything that everyone had ever asked of him, yet he had been unable to maintain even one satisfying personal relationship. He was a failure and a worthless person.

Through therapy, Ben was able to understand that he and his siblings were peripheral people in his family of origin. All of the children—but most especially Ben, as he was the only boy—were clearly expected to be high achievers in order to vicariously meet their parents' needs for esteem. They were expected, in fact, to anticipate all the needs of their parents (a blatantly impossible task) and to provide for them, or else they were severely punished for their "selfishness," "stupidity," and "ingratitude."

Ben told a story about coming home from school one day when he was in the fourth or fifth grade. His family lived in a coastal town where they rarely saw snow. It had snowed during the day, however, and he and his sisters and friends were outside playing in it when their father arrived home. In spite of the fact that this was the first snowfall in many years, and that Ben had not been told to shovel the snow (nor had he ever used a shovel), the father was furious that Ben had not cleared the driveway; he yelled at Ben and hit him. Ben was reduced to tears in front of his sisters and friends, more from the absolute injustice and frustration of the situation than from the physical pain. When he went in the house later, after shoveling the rapidly melting snow ("It was gone by the next morning, anyway!" he remembers), his mother was totally unsympathetic to his feelings, instead conveying disgust and disapproval at him for upsetting his father.

As Ben told the story twenty years later, he still became furious: "He called me selfish and stupid. Can you believe that? *He* said that to *me*! Him! The most selfish, stupid bastard on the face of the earth! God, I hate him!" It is a perfect example of how the narcissistic parent system operates to undermine self-confidence and impair decision-making ability. Ben, as an adult, was unable to set boundaries in his life essentially because he was not trained as a child to believe that he had that option.

People Pleasing

Individuals who undergo years of this deficient kind of training can become "people pleasers" (an Alcoholics Anonymous term) to the extreme. Because they were never allowed to establish limits as children, they are unable to do it as adults. They may be able to set reasonable boundaries in some areas of their lives, usually those areas that were not subject to "training" by their families of origin (such as on-the-job situations). These same individuals, as illustrated in the case below, may be completely unable to do it in other areas—usually family and other interpersonal relationships, where the "training ground" was in the narcissistic home.

Kate's Story.   Kate is an administrator for a large public institution. In the work environment, she functions superbly: her decisions are appropriate, and she has no difficulty in delegating work to her staff, in making kind but firm corrective statements, in advocating her views with her superior, in maintaining a warm but detached relationship with her staff, or—when necessary–in firing personnel. In other words, her boundaries are well in place in her professional life.

In her personal life, however, she has virtually no boundaries. As a divorced mother, she runs herself ragged doing things for her twelve-year-old daughter that the daughter could do very well for herself (laundry, shopping, lunch preparations, transportation to the mall when they are on a direct bus line, and so on). As the "responsible" daughter in a highly dysfunctional narcissistic family, Kate feels she must be "on call" twenty-four hours a day to take care of her parents' and grown siblings' needs.

In her relationships with men, she has no idea how to indicate her own appropriate needs for respect and nurturing, and how to set boundaries on the behaviors she will tolerate. As a result, she found herself having unwanted sex with every man she dated, and then loathing herself. She finally decided it was easier not to date at all, so this very attractive, intelligent woman found herself alone and lonely every Saturday night (when her daughter stayed with the father).

All or Nothing

The inability to set reasonable boundaries often results in the "all or nothing" syndrome. Most therapists have seen patients who would rather just divorce their spouse than sit down and discuss how some changes could be made in the relationship. Or the adolescent who will not answer the phone because someone they do not like is going to ask them for a date, and they do not know how to say no. Or the man who would rather quit his job than ask his boss for a raise. If these individuals cannot have a perfect relationship, with another person intuitively knowing how to meet their needs (the "all" part), then they would rather cut their losses and divorce, or quit, or stay incommunicado—that is, not have the relationship at all (the "nothing" part).

These patients are neither incredibly stupid nor as impossibly resistant as they often seem to their therapists, who may have difficulty dealing with this "Yes, but . . ." class of patient.[3] What these individuals are, however, are people who cannot recognize the legitimacy of their feelings and needs—who cannot self-validate—so they genuinely cannot fathom the possibility of sitting down with a spouse, friend, colleague, or whomever and having a reasonable discussion to set boundaries so that those feelings and needs can be accommodated.

Responsibility and Control

As mentioned earlier, adults raised in narcissistic families tend to take on responsibility for things they do not control. They see no logical inconsistency in this, as it conforms so well to their worldview. It is difficult for them to master the concept that assuming responsibility for something without being in control of it is inviting craziness—or, at least, inviting failure, self-loathing, and feelings of worthlessness. Two techniques that we have found helpful in teaching this concept are "the notebook" and "world crisis."

The Notebook

During therapy sessions, I usually take process notes in stenographic notebooks. When patients are having difficulty grasping the concepts of setting boundaries and responsibility/control, I hold out the notebook and say, "Take this." They are surprised by the command, but they always take the notebook. I sit back, cross my arms, and wait. After the patient has sat there looking puzzled for a few seconds, I ask them why they wanted the notebook. Of course, they can not come up with an answer right away (since it is not a legitimate question), but eventually they will say something to the effect that they did not want the notebook, but I told them to take it, so they did. I ask, "What are you going to do with the notebook?" (By now they are starting to feel a little uncomfortable, wondering if their therapist is, as we say in Rhode Island, "one clamcake short of a dozen.") They stammer, and they exhibit emotions ranging from embarrassment to confusion to irritation to anger. Then I ask them, "Do you want the notebook?" By now, of course, they wish they had never seen the notebook—or me. After eliciting various protestations about the notebook, I ask, "Would you like to give the notebook back to me?" Needless to say, they can not wait to get rid of it.

I explain that the notebook represents responsibility, that there are all kinds of options that are available when someone asks you to "take the notebook." We explore some of those options, such as finding out the following information:

- Why are you giving it to me?
- For how long?
- What's in the notebook?
- Can I do whatever I want with it?
- How heavy is it?
- If I take it, will I own it?
- Why don't you want it anymore?
- Is it dangerous to have the notebook?
- Will someone else want the notebook and try to take it from me?
- Do you have the right to give it away? Do you own it?

Patients also see that they can formulate *conditions* under which they will take the notebook:

- For a few minutes
- Until it gets too heavy
- If I can read it
- If you pay me (this one gets used a lot!)

They can also say no—with or without explanation. They are encouraged to come up with statements for refusal that are respectful and adult, not excuses (like "I feel sick"). Some statements patients have devised are as follows:

- I don't want to
- It's not a good time for me
- I'm cutting back on notebook taking
- I gave up taking notebooks for Lent

My personal favorite, which I often teach to survivors, is *"I think not, but thank you for asking"*—which is probably the quintessential refusal statement.

Holly's Story.   Holly, an adult child of a covertly narcissistic family, had been working diligently in therapy to understand her difficulty in the area of boundary setting. She knew that she gave out mixed messages because of her problems with self-validation and her strong need for approval. A financially strapped single mother, Holly was trying to establish herself as a free-lance illustrator. In the course of making contact with potential customers, she was taken to lunch by the art editor for an important catalog publisher. He was very complimentary of her work, and he behaved in an entirely professional manner. Although she had been initially nervous about the lunch meeting, particularly about her ability to stay in her "professional adult mode" and not give the man any messages that her intentions for the lunch were other than strictly business, Holly found herself gradually relaxing and enjoying herself.

Her companion was intelligent and witty, and he made no secret of the fact that he was married and the father of four. He talked at length about his family, especially about his children, whom he missed; his schedule necessitated his separation from them during the week (he stayed in the city, and they remained at home two hours away). Holly found the family talk reassuring, and she felt that the lunch was going well. Toward the end of the meal, the editor, who was in the position to direct a great deal of work toward Holly, started to talk about his art collection. Warning bells went off in Holly's head, but she ignored them. Then, at the close of the lunch, the editor casually put his hand on her arm and announced, as though it were a sudden inspiration, "Say, why don't we stop off at my place for coffee, and you can see my collection firsthand!" Holly, seeing her potential income going up in smoke should she offend the editor—but unwilling to pay the price he was evidently suggesting—removed his hand from her arm. She gave him a vigorous handshake, her biggest smile, and a hearty "I think not, but thank you for asking," then beat a hasty retreat to her car.

When Holly discussed the incident in therapy, she felt proud of herself that she had (1) been able to refuse, (2) refused without trying to ingratiate herself in some other way, and (3) not made up an excuse. As a postscript, the editor never did call—but his superior, seeing Holly's work in a local newspaper, did. She was thus able to feel good about herself and to get work on her own terms.

(On the lighter side, another patient tells a funny—and true—story about being in Grand Central Station in New York City, waiting for a train, when a disreputable-looking drunk staggered up to her, looked her up and down, and said loudly, "Want to f—-?" Without missing a beat, she replied, "I think not, but thank you for asking!" She felt pretty good about herself, too!)

To return to the notebook example, I then discuss the concept of responsibility, and explain to the patients that all the options they came up with taking the notebook are available to them in terms of assuming *any* kind of responsibility. They usually get it, with the kind of "Aha!" response that is the equivalent of a light bulb turning on.

World Crisis

I move directly from the notebook to a "world crisis" exercise. By now the patient is relaxed and is having fun, so she or he is open to more games.

I choose a current situation in the world and tell the patient that she or he is responsible for the outcome. For instance, during the 1992 presidential election I asked patients who they wanted to win the election. Many said Bill Clinton. I then told them. "Let's say, just for the sake of argument, that I tell you to make it happen. I tell you further, that it is your *responsibility* to see that he gets elected. If he doesn't, it is your fault. I am instructing you to go out and get Clinton elected. Do you see any problem with that?"

After some discussion, patients are able to pretty easily identify that there is indeed a problem: they do not have the power to accomplish the task. They do not control the direction of the campaign, the media coverage, who will vote, the weather on election day, behavior at the polling places, or how those who go to the polls will cast their vote. As much as they might want to, they just cannot do it. I then ask them if it would be fair or reasonable to blame them if (in the above illustration) Clinton did not win. They can see that it would not be their fault.

It is patently unrealistic to assume responsibility for situations or conditions that one does not control. Once patients understand and internalize this concept, it is enormously liberating for them. During their childhood they were constantly made to feel responsible for things they did not control, and they have carried that perception with them into adulthood, incorporating it into their worldview. To understand finally and feel that they do not have to do that anymore is powerful.

Learning How to Set Boundaries

Comfort with setting boundaries develops naturally in children who have their feelings respected by their parents. In this context, children are allowed to participate in decisions that affect them, are encouraged to talk about their feelings, and get validation for the appropriate expression of them without needing to resort to shouting and/or tears if the decision does not go their way. In other words, the children learn to use the "I feel . . . I want" format (see Chapter Five).

The children learn not only to tune in to their own and other people's feelings, but that they can live with the occasional disapproval of others. This is an important lesson. It is difficult for most people to elicit disapproval—to say, in effect, "I'd like to be able to meet your needs, but I can't. In this case, our needs are in conflict, and I have to attend to mine. I have to say no." It is important for patients to understand that, while it is a difficult skill to acquire, it is vital to our mental health and positive self-image that we learn to be advocates for ourselves. Otherwise, we end up meeting other people's needs at the expense of our own. If we are further able to communicate our message in a respectful and adult way, people will be able to hear our message clearly without being threatened or devalued by it.

If this is a tall order for a reasonably healthy adult, it is a herculean task for a youngster. It is made immeasurably easier if the child learns the following at home:

1. Correction, appropriately expressed, is not destructive, hurtful, or shame inducing.
2. One's needs cannot always be met by others, they but can always be appropriately articulated to others.

3. Feelings do not need justification—one always has a right to one's feelings.

4. One does not always have the right to act out on one's feelings: all actions have consequences, and these need to be thought about.

5. Compromise means giving up as well as getting.

6. Changing one's mind is not necessarily a bad thing; part of growing up is the ability to react based on new information.

7. Making mistakes is often how we learn. There is no shame involved.

8. Being able to "own" our mistakes, apologize if appropriate, and make amends where possible, is how we grow. "I'm sorry; tell me what I can do to make it up to you" is a statement of strength, not an admission of weakness or shame.

If children are fortunate enough to grow up in a home where these eight rules are acted out in the course of daily events, they will probably be healthy, secure adults with positive self-images. They will probably be comfortable with their feelings and have little difficulty with setting reasonable boundaries in their lives.

Actions First . . . Feelings Follow

But what of the children raised in narcissistic families? What of the Bens and Kates, with limited confidence in their ability to assess the appropriateness of their actions and decisions? An essential part of therapy with these individuals involves retraining. What they did not get as a child from their parents, they can get as an adult from themselves: once they understand how they were mistrained, they can make the decision to retrain. They can, in adulthood, make a conscious decision to incorporate these eight rules into their lives and act as if they believed them. When one acts "as if" for long enough, eventually it becomes part of one's belief system.

Feelings always follow actions. It is imperative when working with these patients to reinforce this premise continually. The patients cannot wait to feel more confident in order to act more confidently—to make firm decisions, to be advocates for themselves, to set rules and boundaries for themselves and the way they wish to be treated. They can check out the appropriateness of their decisions with the therapist, of course, but they need to act "as if" they believe in themselves before they can feel that belief and confidence. The actions come before the feelings; with time, however, the feelings will follow.

Conclusion

The challenge in helping patients to deal with issues of power and control is to assist them in beginning to set appropriate boundaries in their lives—a difficulty with many adults from narcissistic families. It can be threatening to them, as well as frustrating for the therapist. There are a lot of opportunities for the client to get stuck, since concepts of limit setting strike at the heart of what most survivors were taught. Without the ability to limit and order their lives, however, patients will not be able to progress in therapy.

7
Decision Making and Deferment of Gratification

A dults who have been raised in either overtly or covertly narcissistic family systems have learned not to trust. They may
have a series of behaviors that they label as trust or trusting—
including injudicious self-disclosure, immediate and total belief in
what another person tells them without the history to support it, or
the naive belief that another person may be able to meet all their
needs or solve all their problems—but when these relationships fall
apart (as they invariably do), they revert to their worldview: "I can't
trust anyone, because whenever I do, I get hurt."

Genuine trust is something that is learned in childhood. The narcissistic family, of course, is not a good place to learn trust, as children are not given the opportunity to learn about their feelings and
needs in any consistent way and so cannot learn to be trusting of
themselves—of their validity, perceptions, character, uniqueness,
abilities, or worth. Without essential trust (trust in oneself), decision
making that involves the ability to do long-range planning (which is
based on postponement of gratification) becomes difficult. To work
toward a goal without some immediate payback means that one has
faith in the eventual outcome: trust in oneself to make it happen,
and trust in others not to "change the rules" or present insurmount-
able obstacles.

In the narcissistic family, things happen more or less on the whims of the parent(s). Promises are made, but they may not be kept. Further, it is difficult for the child to make any predictions about whether a particular promise will be kept, because he or she does not understand that the basis for parental decision making is meeting the needs of the parent(s). Consider the example below:

Billy: Dad! Mom! I've got my baseball schedule. Can you guys come to all my games this year?

Dad: Sure, sport. Wouldn't miss the chance to see my boy be a star!

Billy: Dad, I'm not exactly a star. I play outfield.

Dad: Well, you work hard, and soon you'll be the pitcher.

Billy: Did you mean what you said about coming to all the games? Really?

Dad: Of course I did. Whenever I can.

Billy: Mom, too?

Dad: Jeez, Billy . . . I'd said we'd be there.

The promise is that Dad and Mom will go to all of Billy's baseball games. This promise is repeated every game for five games; two games it is kept, the other three it is not. Billy cannot predict if his parents will actually be at any given game, because they always promise to be there but often are not. He does not understand why they come or do not come. It does not seem to relate to the weather, as one of the times they showed up it was sunny, but the other time it was raining. It does not relate to sickness either, as the sunny time Mom had a bad cold but came anyway. Billy learns from this that he cannot trust long-range plans, his parents' word, his ability to positively influence his environment and therefore himself.

What Billy does not understand is that on the occasions when Mom and Dad came, their needs and his accidentally coincided. The time Mom came with a bad cold, she and Dad were meeting friends at the game. The time they went in the rain, they saw themselves as "super parents" who would be approved of by the coach for being there in bad weather. The times they did not go, it was because there was no payoff for them. Because they did not want to go they made excuses, they apologized, they asked for Billy's understanding, and they became irritable and ultimately angry when he did not understand. At no time did Billy's parents seriously consider his need to have them there, or his need to be able to count on their keeping their word. Thus he was never able to relax or make plans, because of his parents' apparent inconsistency and unpredictability.

In a healthy family system, Billy's parents would have asked him about his wishes concerning their attendance, validated his expressed need (whatever it was), and talked realistically about their own limitations. Contrast the way Johnnie's parent handles the same situation:

Johnnie: It's going to be such a great year! We've got the best team in the league! I know we'll be in the playoffs this year! You and Dad'll be at my games, won't you?

Mom: You like to have us there a lot, don't you? It's nice for parents to know they're wanted!

Johnnie: It's more fun when I know you're out there. It makes me feel—important, sort of.

Mom: You are important—sort of!

Johnnie: (*laughing*) Well, can you come to all my games?

Mom: I don't know about all, honey. It depends on how many are during work. I have an idea: why don't you go get your schedule, and we can look at it and write the games on the kitchen calendar. Then we'll be able to plan who can go to which games. Okay?

Johnnie: Yeah. That's a good idea. But what about games when you're working?

Mom: Well, why don't you think of something so that those games make you feel important, too?

Johnnie: Like what?

Mom: Do I look like I'm Johnnie? You tell me!

Johnnie: Well . . . you mean like . . . taking a friend? Or, going out for pizza after?

Mom: Yes. Stuff like that. I'm sure we'll be able to work something out. By the way—I'll still be really proud of you, even if you don't make the playoffs. I'm proud of you right now.

In this scenario, Johnnie has been encouraged to express his feelings and wishes, and he has had them validated by his mother. He has been treated respectfully and realistically. He knows what he can count on—it is posted on the calendar. He has not been ignored, nor has he been promised the world. He knows that he is valued for himself, not just for his achievements. He has been given the opportunity to make some plans for himself. If his parents stick to this schedule most of the time, Johnnie will learn to trust in them, in himself, and in long-range payoffs.

The Billys of this world, however, may not develop that essential trust. Billy may learn that, like the song says, "tomorrow never comes": if you really want something, you had better grab it right now![1]

The Quick Fix

Dysfunctional families produce people who need immediate gratification—the "quick fix." These individuals have no faith in their ultimate ability to prevail, so they look for immediate ways to make themselves feel better; food, alcohol, spending money, and sex are the most common. All of these "fixes" can lead to feelings of self-loathing and depression, which lead to the need for more fixes to lift the depression, which lead to more depression. As one patient put it, "I had to drink to solve the problems caused by drinking."

In an age of thirty-second television solutions, unrealistic body images, real-life random violence (even at elementary schools), no meaningful gun control, media and entertainment industry preoccupations with sex and violence, nuclear accidents, institutionalized discrimination, police forces out of control, and the decline of both organized religion and the nuclear family, the quick fix is not only encouraged—it looks pretty good. This is especially true for adults from narcissistic homes; those individuals we have treated all have problems with delaying gratification, and all have problems with at least one of the "big three": alcohol and drugs, food, and overspending. After all, in a chaotic and frightening universe, one counts on what one can most easily control.

Even in the early 1900s, Jung was writing about his concerns with the direction in which society was moving: away from spiritual grounding and toward self-destructive behaviors.

All ages before us have believed in gods in some form or other. Only an unparalleled impoverishment of symbolism could enable us to rediscover the gods as psychic factors, that is, as archetypes of the unconscious.[2]

Linking Jung's theories to the increasing presence of oral addictions (eating disorders, alcohol abuse, smoking) gives those of us in the mental health field much food for thought (pun not intended). We would enlarge this thesis to include the narcissistic family. Within this family structure, it is not possible for the child to have faith in the constancy and predictability of his parents' actions, as he is in ignorance of their motivations. He is, then, uniquely positioned to develop belief in only what he can externally control—like food, drugs, spending, and sex.

A significant number of the adults we treat from narcissistic family systems are bulimic. Their more usual pattern is not binge and purge, but rather binge and diet. They need the quick fix, so they binge; then they feel guilty and ashamed, so they starve. They then feel deprived and depressed, so they eat again to feel better. Because they are externally motivated and have little sense of their inherent worth, they look at pictures of models or women on television and feel unattractive, so they starve again. With many of these patients, this is a lifetime pattern of eating.[3] They are usually reluctant to bring it up in therapy. They rationalize that it is not dangerous, because they do not vomit. We believe they are also afraid that the therapist will make them give it up, and they do not know any other way to live. It is important for therapists who work with these individuals to revisit, in therapy, their patterns in the "big three" areas, as it is often only when a solid therapeutic relationship has been established that the patients can overcome their shame at disclosing such dysfunctional behaviors.

Distortion of Reality

Because of their lack of essential trust, many patients from narcissistic homes have no faith either in long-range goals or in their ability to sustain those goals. Low self-esteem compounds the problem. Then, as if all that were not difficult enough to deal with, they frequently have seriously distorted views of reality. They tend to see others as more attractive, more capable, more *everything* than they are. It is inconceivable to them that anyone else feels insecure, or unpopular, or fat, or any other sense of being "less than" than they themselves feel. It is ironic that adults who were raised in narcissistic families are never more egocentric than in their preoccupation with their inferiority! They are certain that they are especially, uniquely defective—that while other people may occasionally make mistakes, it is only *they* whose mistakes are unforgivable. These individuals really believe this, and really believe all the fairy tale, Brady Bunch (or Cosby family) stuff about "other people's families." When they have difficulty coping, they are usually certain that anyone else, in a similar situation, could have—*would* have—done it much better.

Therefore, as we mentioned in Chapter Four, reality testing is a significant part of therapy with these patients. It is amazing to learn about the erroneous assumptions they make, against which they measure themselves and come up lacking.

> **Barbara's Story.** Barbara is a fifty-year-old librarian who entered therapy for generalized anxiety disorder. She was raised in a relatively high-functioning ethnic household where the boys were treated like princes and the girls as if they were invisible.
>
> The adult child of a covertly narcissistic family, Barbara could never remember receiving any praise. She was a straight-A student, went to college on full scholarship, got a job upon graduation, and continued working as she got married and had two children. When she got divorced, she raised the children by herself. Both turned out well; Barbara never asked her parents for help, and never was any offered. She was still being "the good daughter" (visiting the parents every Sunday, doing their grocery shopping, taking care of them when they were sick) and trying to get praise from her parents when she entered therapy.
>
> Barbara progressed rapidly in therapy, and it was in her termination visit that she "confessed" her most shameful truth—she had no intimate women friends. Her therapist was surprised, to say the least, at this revelation, as Barbara appeared to have a large circle of women friends, often reporting tennis dates, lunch dates, shopping trips—all kinds of social events, as well as frequent telephone contact. When

questioned, Barbara got teary, and she talked about a movie called *An Unmarried Woman* that she had seen in the early 1970s.[4] According to Barbara, in this movie the heroine, a woman in the process of divorce, had a group of three women friends she met every Friday night at the same restaurant, and they told each other *all* the intimate details of their lives, and they were there for each other *all* the time. No matter what else was going on in their lives, this group of friends met and were entirely, 100 percent emotionally available for each other.

From seeing this 120-minute piece of Hollywood make-believe, Barbara had drawn conclusions about her own self-worth and relationships: she was not a good friend, she had no real friends, and all other women had friendships like the ones she had seen in the movie. Twenty years later, this intelligent, educated woman was astonished to learn that that simply was not true. Not only did all other women *not* belong to a group like that, but her therapist did not know of *any* other women who did. Barbara left the session on top of the world. It was good not to have pervasive anxiety any more, but it was even better to find out that she had so many good friends! It was probably the most helpful information Barbara got from therapy, and it very nearly did not happen.

Unrealistic Expectations

As seen in Barbara's story, a distorted worldview often leads adults from narcissistic families to have unrealistic expectations for themselves and for others. When they combine this with their lack of trust in long-term payoffs and their inability to set realistic boundaries, these people frequently characterize themselves as quitters, procrastinators, or lazy. Their already low self-esteem is further lowered because they seemingly can not carry out a project to completion. Some of the self-descriptions we have heard from patients are as follows:

"I'm an Olympic starter—but I can't finish anything!"
"I'm the queen of unfinished projects."
"I guess I'm just a wimp. When things get tough, I run away."

"I go into projects with so much enthusiasm! But then—I don't know—I just lose interest."

"It's like—I gather up my courage and make a start. But then, as soon as there is the least little problem, or if everyone isn't just standing in line, cheering me on, I lose interest. I get scared. I have to start something else."

"I've made a career out of being number two."

"Maybe I'm a genetic freak. I'm missing the gene for tenacity."

"I hate myself for being so lazy! Everybody else seems to be able to do all this stuff. I try, but I can't. I guess I *am* a lazy slob." (This was her mother's frequent appellation for her.)

Old Unreliable Me

It is interesting, after listening to a patient recite the familiar litany of how she is wimpy, unreliable, weak, and a quitter, to ask her if it is possible that she merely changed her mind. If perhaps, based on information she took in after she started the project (hooked rug, hair dressing course, law school, or the army), she realized that it was not something that suited her needs at that time, and so she terminated it. Perhaps this information might have been difficult to ascertain prior to actually starting and experiencing the project (for example, has anyone ever done a study of medical students who have to drop out because they discover they can not stand the sight of so much blood? How would they have known that prior to medical school?) Perhaps what she did was make a mature, adult judgment based on new information.

In reality, these individuals are not raised to know themselves. They are raised to know others, to be able to predict what others expect of them, and to meet (or fail to meet) that explicit or implicit need. Therefore they try many things for which they are ill suited. At the time of life (childhood and adolescence) when other kids were trying out varying kinds of behaviors, making messes, and learning what works in the world and what does not, these children were taking care of their parents' emotional needs. But while they could not experiment and try new things then, they can now.

The unrealistic expectations (see previous section) held by many adult children from narcissistic families are a further set-up for over-commitment of time and energy. As one of our patients thought, if everyone else can do these things,—work full time, raise two children, keep the house, be treasurer of the PTA, lead a cub scout troop, teach sunday school, run for town council, do all her own baking, *and* finish a master's degree—then she should be able to, also. When it became impossible to accomplish all of the tasks, she then felt inadequate. The reality, though, was that the expectations were unrealistic, not that she was deficient. The job of the therapist in this situation was to mirror reality for the patient and to help her decide (1) which of the commitments were essential, (2) which others provided such a high level of personal satisfaction that it would be counterproductive to give them up, and (3) which could not be continued.

In this case, the patient cited working full time and parenting as essential, and finishing her master's degree as so "soul satisfying" that she truly did not want to give it up. Over a two month period, every other commitment was given up. A system of chores was worked out so that the rest of the family did the cleaning and much of the cooking (not up to her standards, but she had to let go of those, too), she dropped out of the town council race, and she found others to take over her volunteer jobs. She even located a grocery store that carried a good selection of breads. Not surprisingly, the patient found that she *was* able to complete tasks—now that she had a more reasonable number of tasks to complete.

Part of responsible decision making is the ability to change one's mind based on new information. There would be no progress in any field of endeavor if that were not true. It then follows logically that individuals need to recognize that, for any given situation, there are a series of options available for consideration.

Options and Consequences in Decision Making

We commented previously that adults raised in narcissistic families are frequently "all or nothing" people (see Chapter Six). Things are seen in terms of black and white, good and bad, with a moralistic position that presupposes there to be a right (and wrong) answer or solution to virtually every situation. They are metaphorically looking for some cosmic scale that will rate all feelings, thoughts, and actions from one (least acceptable, bad) to ten (most acceptable, good). These are people whose daily vocabulary is peppered with "shoulds." For individuals with this orientation, the concept of making a mistake and either blowing it off or learning from it is utterly foreign. A mistake is a wrong or bad thing, with strong overtones of immorality or even sinfulness. If one makes a mistake, one *is* a mistake; it is yet another example of one's unworthiness and essential deficiency. Feelings are irrelevant. It is doing the right thing—guessing right, meeting other people's needs, and getting approval—that matters.

For these patients, the idea of having a menu of options from which to choose is foreign, if not bizarre. Options are not opportunities for success, they merely multiply one's opportunities for making mistakes. There can be, after all, only one right answer to any given question. (With this attitude, individuals raised in narcissistic families must make poor philosophy students.)

It is a tremendous leap, therefore, within this moralistic, black-or-white thinking construct to recognize that there are options to consider in virtually every situation; that those options carry with them built-in consequences; and that the basis for intelligent decision making rests on measuring the efficacy of each option according to how its consequences will affect oneself—not on how right or wrong it is according to some external standard. Whenever he uses the word *should,* for instance, the patient is considering a decision based on an external standard, rather than on his internal needs. In our practice, we tell patients that "should" really means "I don't want to, but *they* want me to." The "should" decision-making model is well taught in the narcissistic family, where all decisions are based on meeting others' needs rather than one's own.

As we have said, the concept that life is a series of options that carry with them inherent consequences is not part of the cognitive milieu of narcissistic family progeny. They will experience tremendous shame when recalling "bad" or "stupid" things they did in the past, with no understanding that they came to make those decisions because of a lifetime of experiences and training. What really happened was that they made the best choice they could based on the options open to them. These products of narcissistic family systems will undoubtedly have fewer options available to them at any given time than will persons raised in more healthy family situations. In healthy families, youngsters are given increasing discretionary powers for decision making as they grow older, so that they have opportunities for experiencing both failure and success based on decisions they have made freely. This is a concept that is often difficult for patients to understand. It is far easier for them to continue to see themselves as deficient and guilty.

Lennie's Story.   Lennie is a slight, wholesomely pretty twenty-five-year-old woman who works as an office manager for a small computer software company. At age sixteen she was living at home (a poor section of a midwestern industrial city) with her factory-worker father, housewife mother, and three brothers. One night she went into a bar on a dare from her friends. There she met a twenty-four-year-old man named Bill. Bill paid a great deal of attention to her that night, followed her home, and later showed up at her school, ultimately seducing her and pressuring her into running away with him. He took her to the Southwest, where they lived with his preschool-age son by a previous marriage. During the almost seven years they were together (they eventually married), he beat and raped her, isolated her with the child, and forbade her to have any friends or to contact her family. During that time, Lennie's family made no move to find or to contact her.

It became clear to Lennie after several years that Bill "had problems with alcohol and cocaine." When the son entered the fourth grade, Lennie was able to convince her husband to let her go to work. Through work she hooked up with a friend who took her to Al-Anon meetings during lunch breaks, and over time Lennie was able to realize that she was in a destructive situation, move out, and file for divorce.

When Lennie entered therapy, she was overwhelmed with shame and suffering from severe depression. She wanted to find out "what was wrong"—which really meant why *she* was wrong—so that she would not get into another bad relationship. Through therapy, Lennie finally allowed herself to experience the loss of her stepson (although she had raised him from age three to age ten, as a stepparent she had no rights, even for visitation). She was then encouraged by her therapist to explore other losses she might have suffered in her lifetime.

Although she was able to mourn the loss of her son and to acknowledge that she had a right to mourn him, Lennie was still unable to look at her own childhood and adolescence with anything but shame. She was overwhelmed with the loss of her adolescence. The only conclusion she could reach about herself was that she was stupid, bad, and defective. The idea that running away with Bill was a judgment she made based on (1) her life experiences up to that point and (2) the options available to her at that time was inconceivable to her.

In order to help patients like Lennie better conceptualize the difficulty they have in recognizing and considering options, we have developed a teaching tool that we call "The Story of Purple." Lennie's therapist told it to her at this point in the therapy.

The Story of Purple.   Once upon a time, there was a great land called Purple. It was named Purple because everything in it was, in fact, purple! The grass was a deep purple, the sky was a pinkish purple, the cows were pale purple with mauve spots, and the three suns and thirteen moons were purple. The water was pale purple, and the food was in shades of purple ranging from mist lavender to midnight plum. Even the people were varying shades of purple. Everything was purple. In this land, not only were there no other colors, no one even knew that any other colors existed!

Is it likely, do you think, in this land—where everything was as completely purple as purple can possibly be—that one day, a young purple person would get out of her purple bed, but on her purple clothing, and while brushing her purple hair, look in the mirror and announce, "I think I'd look better in green"? [At this point, most patients "get it," and you elicit some laughter.]

The answer is, of course not! *Green is not an option!*

Back to Lennie.   Eventually Lennie was able to understand the dynamics at work in her covertly narcissistic family of origin. Lennie's parents were forced into marriage by an unwanted pregnancy. There was no intimacy in this family, no talking about feelings, and no room for differentness of any sort. The atmosphere in the home was so tense, so thick with unspoken feelings and resentments, that Lennie remembers always wishing that she was not there. She could not wait to leave home.

The role of the children in this narcissistic family was not to make waves, and to live out the expectations of the parents. The parents were determined that their children were going to have a "better life than we've had," but they actively resented their children; both parents were martyrs-by-choice to the family. The sons had a number of opportunities available to them, but the daughters had only two options available: either (1) they graduated from high school, lived at home, went to the local community college, and did the housework; or (2) they graduated from high school, got married, went to live in their husband's home, and did the housework.

In role-playing exercises with Lennie, her therapist explored the kind of conversations *another* adolescent girl might have had with her parents. These included the exploration of options such as getting a job, finding a friend with whom to share an apartment and expenses, or just talking about her ambivalent feelings about attending the local community college. Lennie realized that none of those options had been available to her. As it was, she was a bright, creative girl who was stuck in a bad high school in a dead-end neighborhood, who could not imagine four more years of boring classes and of being a maid for her brothers and father. So, option number one (college) was out; that left option number two (a man).

Lennie was able to see that she had actually been trying, with a few permutations, to meet parental expectations by exiting from the family vis-à-vis running away with Bill. She was shocked to realize that this act—which she had always considered incontrovertible proof of her stupidity and badness—was actually a back-door way to fulfill her parental obligations and meet their needs. Had "just moving out, getting a job, sharing an apartment with a couple of girls, maybe taking some night courses at the university" been an option, she would have taken it.

As Lennie said at the end of the "Story of Purple" session: "I've never understood why I ran away with him! I was never a rebellious kid. I was always treated like I was, but I wasn't. I never did anything bad. I was really a good kid! (She is crying by now.) I knew it wasn't love, and I was so scared. When he gave me the ultimatum— 'now or never'— I knew it was crazy. I only had one month to go before graduation. But I thought I had to. I knew I just couldn't go to that dumb college. And the boys I knew . . . ugh! They were immature and boring. I don't know. It seemed like . . . there was no choice for escape . . . Bill was it. My God! If I'd ever thought . . . to be able to get a job and an apartment, I'd have jumped at the chance! I was so stupid . . . no, I wasn't stupid. You're right. I never thought of it, because it wasn't an option. Not in my family. My God, I *wasn't* so stupid. It just wasn't an option."

Conclusion

Patients respond well to the premise that decision making or long-range planning, delaying gratification, project completion—whatever you want to call it—is a learned skill. In this context we use a nonjudgmental, nonblaming approach. It is not that their parents were necessarily bad, but they were unable to teach important skills in this area; we are not talking about a moral failure but about an educational deficit.

Most patients can relate to this. It is not very scary; after all, we all lack skills in some areas. One of the authors of this book is an abominable speller but, fortunately, has a word processor that can check spelling. The other cannot understand how electricity works ("You mean, it isn't magic?") but can hire an electrician.

There are some skills, however, that we need to learn to have a productive life. Task completion (and the ability it implies to defer gratification) is one of them. To the patient, we say, "You didn't learn it then, but you can now. Now you are a grownup, and you have choices and options." We emphasize that good decision making involves looking at every possible alternate to any situation, and then making the decision based on what will be the best option for oneself. One needs to have goals (where I want to be) and then be able to measure options against those goals (will this help me get closer to where I want to be?). If the answer is yes, that is probably the right option at that time.

In the therapy, we stress that there are always risks in decision making. One can make mistakes. In fact, we learn far more from our mistakes than we do from our successes, so mistakes are really learning experiences in disguise. While this may sound a bit Mary Poppins–ish, that does not make it any less true. To take no risks, however, is to stand still—to stay stuck. That, of course, is the biggest mistake, and the pain it causes is usually what brings people into therapy.

When patients can be shown the links between what they experienced as children and what they are doing and feeling now, they are able to feel less defective. They can admit the possibility for change. They can be given the tools for change and be encouraged to take the responsibility to make change happen.

8
Trust and Therapy

Jenny's Story.   Jenny, an attractive, intelligent paralegal, is a married woman with three teenage children. She had entered counseling because of diminished sexual attraction for her second husband and a fear that she would do something "stupid" (like have an affair) to wreck the relationship, as she had with her first marriage. She felt that her life had been a continuing pattern of self-destructive, impulsive acts, and she wanted to find out why while there was still a chance of salvaging the relationship.

Jenny's father was alcoholic and violent. As a low-ranking enlisted man in the military, he was gone for long periods of time, and money was extremely tight. There were seven children in the family; Jenny's mother was abused, poor, overwhelmed, and lonely, and she would "bring men home" during her husband's absences. Jenny has nightmarish childhood memories of drunken brawls between her parents and attempted molestations by her uncle (her mother's brother, whom her mother adored). Seeing her uncle as her mother's only support system, Jenny could not bear to tell her mother about the fondling and deprive her mother of her only ally.

A parentified child from earliest memory, Jenny characterizes her childhood as "always being scared; always just trying to be invisible; trying to be a really good little girl so that no one would notice me and they would just leave me alone." Jenny thus was raised in an overtly narcissistic family.

She remembers a Christmas when she was six or seven years old. Her father had come home on leave two days before Christmas, and on Christmas Eve morning had set out with his brother to get a Christmas tree. The children were, of course, excited about the prospect of having a tree, and they spent the day making decorations for it. The father finally reappeared shortly before midnight, drunk, nasty, and with no tree. A terrible fight ensued between the parents. Jenny remembers huddling in a corner with her younger brother, and believing that if she held him very tightly, they would somehow become one invisible being and would be untouched by the madness and cruelty around them. They stayed there all night, she remembers, with her holding him tightly "for my life—I was protecting him, but holding onto him for dear life!"

In dealing with survivors, the rule is that *the less they got in terms of emotional support from their parents, the more afraid they are to lose the little they have.* For example, Jenny recounts that when she was twelve years old, a horrible, scary mountain man from the Ozarks came to the door to negotiate with her mother for Jenny. He had been visiting relatives in the settlement and had been watching the girl; he wanted to take her home with him as a "wife" for his son. Jenny remembers the terror she felt, listening to her mother talk to the filthy, ignorant, wild-looking stranger who had been leering at her for days every time she went out of the house. She hid in the bathroom with her ear at the door, believing that her mother would sell her—knowing that she would have to kill herself if she did, and afraid that she would not be able to do it quickly or efficiently enough. Jenny's mother did not sell her, but in spite of her protestations that she "never even considered it," to this day Jenny feels that it was a near thing. Even in the face of this and myriad other horror stories, Jenny continues to characterize her mother as "my best friend."

Now, as an adult, Jenny says, "I let people walk all over me. I can't do anything about it. Even if I said something, no one would listen to me. I don't have any close friends. I always do something to push people away. . . . To say that I have an inferiority complex is like saying that Donald Trump's earnings are above the poverty line—it doesn't even come close to describing the enormity of the situation."

After two months of therapy, Jenny came into a session visibly upset. She said that her husband had wanted to make love with her, and she had made an excuse—again. Although he had been hurt and angry, she said that he told her that he was trying to be patient because he knew "that I'm coming in here [to therapy] to get this straightened out, and he knows I'm trying very hard in my therapy and he's sure it'll be better soon. I feel like such a hypocrite! I'm not talking about our sex life; I don't even *care* about our sex life any-more. I haven't had an orgasm in years. I'm just in here talk-ing about me and my past. I mean . . . I know it's all probably related, but how?"

Trust and Intimacy

In Ovid's version of the myth, Narcissus repeatedly tells Echo not to touch him: "Hands off! Embrace me not!"[1] Jenny's story is represen-tative of the way things work in many narcissistic families and why, in adulthood, those survivors have so much difficulty in maintaining intimate relationships. Intimacy is predicated on trust. With trust, one can let people in, drop the defensive stance, and communicate openly. Without trust, there is a "come closer/go away" dance, an "I'll let you in, but not too far or for too long" posture that leads to frustration, hostility, and usually the demise of the relationship.

There are always the exceptions, of course, the spouses and lovers who hang in there in spite of all the mixed messages because they believe the relationship can work. They *are* exceptions, though, and it is extremely difficult to stay in a relationship with someone raised in a narcissistic system (especially a traumatically abusive one) without being negatively affected by him or her. It is difficult, indeed, to be able to detach from the mixed messages without having one's ego bruised, to hear "it's your fault—you do this to me—you expect too much" (or the converse, "It's all my fault—I never do anything right!") over and over again without starting to believe it. The more usual pattern the relationship takes is either that it ends—so that the healthy person can save herself—or that the healthy person becomes affected and the relationship is now survivor/enabler, with the enabler assuming at least part of the responsibility for the survivor's dysfunction. Without the essential element of trust, intimacy cannot happen.

And so we arrive at the issue of trust—trust never learned, or trust unlearned.

The Cycle

The cycle of learning not to trust works something like this for children of narcissistic families:

> I am in pain. There is no one out there to really take care of me. Whenever I allow myself to have feelings, I get hurt. I don't want to feel. I won't feel. I have no feelings. If I can't feel, there's no me. There's no me, but I can watch and adapt. I can lose me, and be who I have to be to survive. Then I can have a relationship. I have a relationship, but I can't trust her (she might hurt me), and I can't trust myself (there is no me). So I can't let her get too close; she might find out there's no me. To protect myself, then, even though I desperately want it, I can't have an intimate and sharing relationship. So I sabotage my relationship. I lose my relationship. I am in pain. [And the cycle repeats.]

Because male/female intimacy frequently implies a sexual relationship, sex often becomes a problem. The topic of sexual dysfunction is discussed in Chapter Nine.

Splitting

One of the ironies of this paradigm is that the quality that enables children to "split" from their feelings and stay alive during their emotionally barren childhoods is the same quality that makes their adulthood so painful. All humans want and need intimacy; to be unable to achieve an intimate relationship is to feel emotionally bereft.

Adults raised in narcissistic families learn to split from their feelings. The ability to develop this splitting as a coping mechanism keeps many children alive. To really look at the reality of their situation—to actually see that their fears of abandonment are real, that they are genuinely on their own with no one to fall back on—is to invite childhood suicide. Young children do kill themselves; splitting thus has a very real protective function.

The more severe form of depersonalization or splitting is frequently found in survivors of childhood sexual and physical abuse. A practice specializing in therapy for incest and other forms of adult and childhood sexual assault, will have a disproportionately high percentage of patients with the diagnosis of posttraumatic stress disorder (PTSD), borderline personality disorder, or multiple personality disorder (MPD).[2] The reintegration of the feeling component (emotion, spirit, soul) of the individual with the physical body is long-term, difficult work.

Although both of us are proponents of short-term therapy (for ethical and practical as well as financial reasons), victims of traumatic sexual abuse are usually long-term patients. When these individuals start therapy, they often want to know, "How long is this going to take? The answer we give is 'two to five years.' Interestingly, women will usually accept this answer, while men want to negotiate. So we negotiate it down to eighteen months, and then at eighteen months we renegotiate. It takes two to five years—and longer, though not necessarily on a weekly basis, for some patients. Systematic, long-term childhood trauma produces a whole range of coping mechanisms either not seen in other patients or not seen with the same depth and intensity; these victims of traumatic, overtly narcissistic families may be in and out of therapy for a major part of their lives.

Extreme Coping Mechanisms in Cases of Traumatic Abuse

As previously indicated, children from narcissistic homes are reflective/reactive; that is, they reflect their parent system's needs rather than explore their own, and they therefore develop a behavior style that is reactive rather than proactive. When the parental system includes assaultive abuse (severe beating, rape, or ritualized torture), the reflection/reaction becomes infinitely more complex. Now, instead of just depersonalizing (removing the feeling part from the body part, as a defense against pain), the individual may split *and* fragment (the angry feelings go there, the tender feelings over there, the betrayed feelings back here, the murderous feelings under there, and so forth). In our practice we view this fragmentation—in the absence of psychosis—as a coping mechanism brought on by the abuse.[3]

Therapists increasingly are using the diagnosis of multiple personality disorder with some of these survivors.[4] We believe there is a risk that this symptom (fragmentation) may be inadvertently encouraged and entrenched by treating it as a disorder in and of itself, rather than as a coping mechanism that worked in childhood but needs to be relinquished now.[5] In our practice we see many survivors who come in with fragmented personalities and could justifiably be diagnosed as having MPD—who, in fact, are fearful that they have this disorder. We prefer to treat these individuals under the umbrella of PTSD or borderline personality disorder.

As all seasoned therapists know, some degree of variance in personality is considered normal. In otherwise adequately functioning people, we call this socialization and label it a skill, not a diagnostic category. When the coping mechanism is more dramatic—when the personalities come and go several times in the course of an hour, and when a therapist is shut in a room, alone, with such a person—it can be frightening, especially if the therapist is inexperienced. The tendency for the therapist may then be to attend to the symptom more than it deserves. We know, for example, not to talk to anorexics about food; we talk about weight instead.[6] To talk about food is to summon defensive behavior and entrench the symptom. In our view, so it can be with fragmented personalities—to attend to that symptom disproportionately is to entrench it. Survivors of traumatic abuse are often people with little sense of self, and as such they are highly suggestible. They may present with all manner of mystical beliefs and bizarre symptoms. It is easy, in therapy, for the dissociative coping mechanism developed in childhood to become MPD.

Keith's Story. Keith, a self-described former drug abuser and heavy drinker, is a handsome, athletic-looking man in his late thirties, unmarried with no children. He entered therapy with extreme misgivings, but because he was desperately afraid that he was going insane and would succeed in killing himself. Even though he was miserably unhappy in every area of his life, totally isolated, and unable to think of any reason to stay alive, he did not want to commit suicide.

Keith came from a financially privileged family. Both of his parents held advanced academic degrees: his father was a person of such renown as to have achieved celebrity status in his field of endeavor; whereas his mother was a person of professional prominence in her own field but only worked part-time to be at home for the children. Keith and his four siblings lived what looked like the American dream—famous parents, handsome children, wealth, private schooling, a close-knit family that spent a lot of time together, family vacations, the whole nine yards.

Yet all the children of this "perfect" family had been heavily involved with drugs from early adolescence into adulthood. None of them had graduated from college. Two had been briefly (for less than eighteen months) married and then divorced; three had never married, and none had children. At the time Keith entered therapy, only one of the five adult children was involved in a relationship. The four children who were heterosexual were alone; the fifth had been living as a homosexual for a decade but had recently decided that he was really bisexual, and he was now living with a woman.

Keith believed he was going insane because he felt "presences" in his house, but there was no one there (he lived alone). He had horrible nightmares from which he would awaken screaming, with his bedclothes drenched from sweat, but he could not remember them afterward. He slept with the lights on when he slept at all; he was drinking heavily before bed so that he could relax enough to fall asleep. He felt that he was virtually invisible to other people, yet he also felt that they were laughing at him. He described himself as "having different personalities": "I'm a real tough, mean bastard; no one even speaks to me at work. People I used to know cross the street when they see me coming—really!"

And that is what he looked like, too: eyes like slits, almost reptilian in their blackness; body posture tense and aggressive; hands either gripping the arms of the chair or clenched into fists. His fantasies, dream content, and thought constructs during these periods were brutal and frightening. When this "dark" personality was displayed in therapy, it was difficult and exhausting for the therapist.

It was also difficult, but for different reasons, when the polar opposite of the "dark" side appeared. This personality was so passive that it was like pulling teeth to elicit any reaction other than withdrawal. As he described himself: "I'm a wimp—a pussy. People walk all over me. I can't even work up the nerve to say hello to a woman I see every day on my way to work." At these times, Keith looked small and weak; he sat hunched over, hands clasped protectively in his lap. His voice and posture screamed "victim." Although Keith manifested a number of other personas, these two were the most prevalent. He often switched back and forth between them during sessions.

This was not Keith's first therapist. He had initially gone to another therapist for two sessions; that therapist referred Keith to his current therapist with the comment, "I don't know what's going on here—maybe sexual abuse—but it's definitely out of my area of expertise!" The first therapist's instincts were correct. As therapy progressed, it was revealed that Keith and his siblings had come from a profoundly narcissistic family where they had been sexually abused by both parents, prostituted to friends and colleagues, and also ritually abused. None of them had *any* pretherapy memories of the abuse.

Three weeks into therapy (and into AA), Keith started to remember his dreams and, at his therapist's suggestion, to write them down in a dream journal. Four months into therapy he started having flashbacks. One year into therapy he got a call from his sister, who had also entered therapy: her therapist had asked her if she had been sexually abused, and she had answered 'yes' but did not know why. Did he have any memories? Three years later, four of the five siblings were in counseling and had retrieved many memories of assaultive abuse. They did not share their memories, but at least they validated each other's knowledge that they were abused as children.

Keith came to understand why his personality fragmented, and he started a "feeling journal" to help him identify what he was feeling and how he acted out those feelings. After five years of therapy, Keith looks and acts "normal." He is leading a productive life and is engaged in some healthy activities that bring him pleasure. He does not always feel normal (whatever that is), but he feels better than he ever has. He is drug and alcohol free and is working on meeting a wider range of people than those he sees at his AA and SA meetings and developing a more fulfilling social life. His personality is integrated, he is free from frightening fantasies of malevolent presences, and he has few nightmares.

Some therapists would have named Keith's personalities, talked to them by their different names, and by so doing have entrenched them more deeply. This is not to say that multiple personality disorder is not a valid diagnostic category. Rather, we issue a caution to therapists who work with these survivors: do not rush toward a method of treatment that encapsulates a patient's feelings and may thus solidify and entrench a symptom.

Use of the Narcissistic Family Model with Survivors of Caretaker Sexual Abuse and Incest

Individuals who have been the victims of traumatic abuse, especially caretaker sexual abuse, feel uniquely shameful. The damage done when the person who is supposed to be protecting and nurturing the child is the one abusing him or her is singularly damaging. The person to whom the child would usually turn for comfort when hurt is the person doing the hurting. That is why we now classify sexual molestation by clergy as incest: the priest (or nun, minister, or the like) is set up by the family in the role of—as well as often being called—father (or sister, brother, and so forth). And these individuals' role as spiritual caretaker, as a person of God, sets them apart in importance/validity from all others in the children's lives except their parents or primary caretakers. Adults who were molested by clergy, whether as children or as adults, tend to take on the same degree of responsibility in their victimization as do individuals molested by their parents.

Couching the abuse in terms of a larger framework—the narcissistic family model—can help these patients to feel less stigmatized. They can be helped to see that in their family of origin, for whatever reason, (1) the needs and feelings of the children were not the primary focus, (2) there was a system in operation that set them up for long-term difficulties, and (3) one of the things that can happen to children raised in these systems is sexual abuse.

The reframing of the abuse is helpful. It serves to quantify it, to make it one part of a larger picture, and to make these patients feel less different from others. The feelings of isolation, differentness, and unworthiness experienced by individuals who are victims of incest presents serious problems in therapy; as one patient put it, "I feel like I have a big *I* tattooed on my forehead." Reframing the abuse does not minimize it, but it does let survivors feel "part of" instead of "separate from," and it broadens the focus from what the individual did or did not do to the narcissistic family system itself.

The Role of the Therapist

A self-identified factor in Keith's recovery was his ability to trust his therapist: "You were the first person I let myself trust [since childhood]. . . . You told me I wasn't crazy. You gave me hope." Learning *not* to trust is a painful but highly functional coping mechanism. It is hard to give up a coping mechanism that may have kept you alive. Learning (or relearning) to trust in adulthood then becomes the primary task for the survivor in therapy. One person who is in a good position to teach the survivor that it is safe to trust is the therapist.

Probably the most important functions the therapist performs with survivors are the following:

- Providing consistent approval and support (of the person, not necessarily of her or his actions)
- Modeling open, adult, nonjudgmental communication (including "I feel . . . I want")
- Providing an educational forum for discussion of options and consequences

- Setting parameters of normal versus abnormal, or healthy versus unhealthy, so that the survivor has some standard against which to hold up and evaluate past and present experiences, judgments, and actions
- *Being trustworthy*—returning calls, being on time for appointments, and acting professionally and consistently

The Borderline Patient

Narcissistic families often produce patients with borderline personality disorder. More than 20 percent of our practice is composed of borderline patients, which is higher than the average caseload.[7] Other therapists who deal with a high percentage of adults raised in narcissistic family systems will probably deal with a high percentage of borderline patients as well. As most therapists know, working with even one patient with a borderline personality disorder is extremely taxing; if a therapist has several of these individuals in care simultaneously, it is an invitation to burnout. Because of this, setting parameters (listed above in "The Role of the Therapist") is particularly important and difficult; where trust is such a pervasive problem, the tendency for the patient to test the therapist repeatedly is obvious.

Therapeutic Guidelines

When the patient has a borderline personality, however, the propensity for setting up impossible tests of the therapist's skill, availability, and commitment is exaggerated. It is therefore essential, when dealing with these patients, that the therapist be open about his or her contractual agreement with the patient. This includes clear and assertive discussion of:

- terms of payment;
- number, duration, and frequency of sessions;
- telephone contact;
- emergency availability;
- vacation schedule; and
- off-duty coverage by another therapist.

Since these patients tend to be are all-or-nothing people, they have little skill in boundary setting and may deeply resent the therapist's attempts to impose boundaries on the therapeutic relationship. The therapist must always encourage discussion of and validate the patient's feelings of frustration, anger, resentment, and fear while continuing to insist on the maintenance of the boundaries set out in the patient/therapist contract.

The modeling of appropriate limit-setting behavior is a constant challenge for the therapist. It is also one of the most valuable long-range contributions the therapist can make to the patient, for it is within the safety of the therapeutic relationship that the patient can learn about trust, appropriate boundary setting, respectful adult communication, and how much one can reasonably expect of another person in terms of getting one's needs met.

Transference

Transference is always a more sticky issue when dealing with patients who were sexually abused. These patients are frequently seductive, both in the literal sense and because, more than other patients, they may cast the therapist in the role of "the only person who can save me." While this is nonsense (there are many competent therapists), it can be flattering and engaging.

It is therefore especially important that the therapist behave in a manner that does not encourage fantasies of a "special relationship" between therapist and patient. Safety issues need to be seriously considered, for the sake of both patient *and* therapist. Obviously, social or sexual contact is prohibited by ethical stands, common sense, and increasingly by law. There are more subtle things that may present difficulties for the patient, however, in that they may give mixed messages and cause anxiety.

While most therapists are well aware of the more obvious 'do's and don'ts' regarding ethical and legal therapeutic behavior, there are more subtle behaviors that can cause problems in the therapeutic relationship. Since both of us spend considerable time doing supervision, we are aware that some of these potentially problematic behaviors are not adequately addressed in many clinical training programs, either classroom or internship. That is why they have been included here as valid considerations in working with all adults raised in narcissistic family systems, but especially when working with survivors of traumatic abuse.

1. Don't see patients at a time when you are alone in the office suite. It can frighten the patient in terms of his or her personal safety, or it can encourage the patient to have fantasies about a possible sexual or "special" relationship with the therapist. It can also be risky for the therapist. Should an angry or confused patient make charges of sexual misconduct, it is more difficult for the therapist to refute those charges if there is no one else around; and should the patient become extremely disturbed or threatening during the session, there is no one who can provide assistance.

2. Don't touch a patient—ever—without asking his or her permission; this includes shaking hands. Adults raised in narcissistic families have difficulty setting personal boundaries. While they may be unable to verbalize that they do not like being touched, that does not mean that they do not *feel* that it frightens them, that the therapist may expect sexual contact, or that all forms of physical touch are assaultive. One of the things the therapist can do for the survivor is to model for them that the survivor owns his or her body and has every right to dictate by who, when, and how he or she can be touched.

3. Be careful about hugging, even if the patient asks for it. Some therapists have a very good sense of when and how to hug patients so that it is appropriate, nurturing, nonsexual, and helpful. Most therapists do not. Always go in the direction of greatest safety for both therapist and patient; *when in doubt, don't.* There is less harm done by following the traditional route of making no physical contact with the patient than by making inappropriate contact.

There are safety issues involved here for both patient and therapist. In our practice some of us are huggers, but most are not. Hugging can easily encourage sexual and 'special-relationship' fantasies on the part of the patient. Further, the fact that a patient wanted to be hugged once does not mean that it will not cross a boundary the next time he is hugged. That 'next hug' can feel unwanted, invasive, or assaultive, so hugging "at the end of every session" or "when the patient cries" or on any kind of ritualized basis can present problems for the patient.

It can also present problems for the therapist. Overinvolvement can easily occur in therapy, and when physical touching between patient and therapist occurs—in any form—it can present boundary issues for the therapist. As patients fantasize about "special" relationships with their therapist, the converse is also true. It is in no one's best interest if the therapist becomes emotionally involved with the patient; if touching is facilitating emotional involvement, it needs to stop.

Taking Care of the Therapist

There are a number of articles and books in development that deal with the topic of burnout and care of the therapist (see Bibliography). We strongly recommend that therapists who work with survivors of assaultively narcissistic families avail themselves of these and other resources. In our experience, therapists do not take good care of themselves. If they are in private practice, they do not schedule reasonable time for meals and recreation. They schedule time for their patients, and often for their spouses and children, but rarely for themselves to be alone, to meditate, to be peaceful.

It is important to remember that one of the critical functions therapists perform is to model the skills they wish their patients to learn. Part of helping patients to trust themselves is learned by their growing trust in their therapist and *her ability to take care of herself*. Recently, one of us had to cancel a group therapy session because of illness. When the group reconvened the next week, a number of the members (all from narcissistic homes) commented on how glad they were about the cancellation. They were personally disappointed that the group was not meeting, but they felt that the therapist was demonstrating self-care—a skill that they were trying to learn. "Physician, heal thyself" is important advice for therapists.

9
Intimacy, Sex, and Friendship

While issues of trust and intimacy have been discussed at length elsewhere in the book (see Chapter Eight), the issue of sexual intimacy deserves separate examination. Remember Jenny's story in the previous chapter? Jenny could not understand how her childhood experiences could impact her adult sexuality, especially when she had experienced years of "normal" sexual interaction with a number of men. What Jenny did not understand is that there is a world of difference between recreational or procreational sex, and sex as an expression of deep feeling and commitment. As the heroine in a recent best-seller says, "In some ways, loving is easy. It's *trusting* that's so hard."[1] Our corollary to that is that sex may be easy, but intimacy is hard.

Like many adults who grow up in narcissistic families, Jenny was able to have a satisfactory sexual relationship with her husband in the early years of their courtship and marriage. It was a very intense time, and the passionate, roller-coaster nature of the relationship made sex exciting. When the relationship evolved into jobs, children who were older and independent, and a husband who had settled down and was looking for a committed relationship, Jenny panicked. Her ability to reach orgasm disappeared, followed shortly by loss of sexual desire.

Jenny was capable of sexuality, but not of intimacy. In the initial stages of male/female survivor relationships, sexuality tends to be stressed to the detriment of intimacy. In cases where the significant other pushes for intimacy, the relationship often ends. Sexuality is often something that adults from narcissistic systems do well, because a big part of being a desirable sexual partner involves being able to be a *reflection* of the other's desires and being able to *react* appropriately—that is, being a reactive/reflective person. When relationships mature (and move out of what a colleague of ours calls the "white heat" stage), then healthy relationships move in the direction of intimacy.

Sexual Counseling: A Crisis of Comfort

For the therapist who may be asked to do sexual counseling with narcissistic family offspring, the initial assessment is often tricky, because the nature of the sexual problems is far less important than the quality of the friendship. If the couple cannot relate well as friends who have open, trusting communication, then sexual counseling will most certainly fail.

It is appropriate at this point to discuss therapeutic options concerning the performance of sexual therapy. As some therapists choose to specialize in work with children and families, some with perpetrators, and some with schizophrenics, so some therapists are drawn to and comfortable with sexual counseling. It is not for everyone. As one of our therapists commented during a peer supervision workshop, "I love to *do* it [be sexual], but I can't *talk* about it like you do! I don't see how you can talk about this stuff [oral sex] with patients!"

Just because therapists have no personal sexual hang-ups does not mean that it is a topic they necessarily enjoy discussing in depth with patients, and enjoyment is important. If the therapist is comfortable, the patients will be; if she is uncomfortable, they will sense it and feel reluctant to pursue in-depth discussions. Even worse, patients may interpret the therapist's discomfort as proof that there really *is* something wrong with them sexually—they are sick, perverted, defective, and so forth.

There is probably no area that is as difficult for couples to talk about as sex. In our society, sex is charged with so many emotional values—moral, performance, and identity—that couples often come into sexual counseling almost physically ill at the prospect of being emotionally "stripped naked" in front of a counselor and being told that what they are doing (or, as they see it, what they have and what they are) is inadequate. *Perceived sexual failure is perceived personal failure.* That is how strongly individuals feel about sexual performance. When they initiate sexual counseling, they come into the first session so uptight it is almost painful to see.

Therefore, if the therapist is also nervous or feeling uncomfortable, it is a set-up for failure. The patients will start to respond in ways that will soothe (in other words, please) the therapist. They will become reactive/reflective instead of responding honestly (that is, being advocates for themselves, and getting their needs met), and they will probably drop out of therapy after the first few sessions.

In our practice, however, we have observed that if the therapist enjoys this work, finding it exciting and even fun, he will soon be able to put patients at ease, validate their feelings of anxiety through normalizing them, and conduct the initial session so that it really is interesting and enjoyable. The patients will leave thinking, "Gee, that wasn't so bad after all," and they will return the next week. They will not feel like degenerates, freaks, or failures, and they will have hope.

In our view, sex counseling is like most therapy: it is 30 percent skill, 30 percent training, and 40 percent alchemy. If the therapist feels embarrassed or uneasy discussing sexual topics (for example, techniques of oral sex, clitoral stimulation, sexual fantasies, pornography, homosexuality, masturbation, and so forth) with patients, and in-depth sexual counseling appears to be necessary, it is possible to refer the couple to a colleague for that "piece" of the therapy. The referral is made with the clear understanding of both your colleague and your patients that they will be referred back to you when that "piece" is finished.

In our group practice, we sometimes do sexual counseling as a team (usually male/female). Within this construct, a more experienced or comfortable therapist can be paired with one who is less experienced or comfortable. Although the less experienced therapist may be uneasy at first, he or she can benefit by modeling the relaxed, forthright techniques of the co-therapist. It is also common in our practice for therapists to refer couples (or individuals) to another therapist for a limited number of sessions specifically for sexual counseling, as described above. We also commonly refer couples to other therapists for marital counseling or couples' groups. When the issues about which the patients were referred out have been resolved, the couple or individual returns to the original therapist.

Our personal bias is in the direction of group practice, because the patients can be better served by having access to therapists with expertise in specialized areas. Cross-referral is so common in our practice that patients are often apprised of the possibility in early sessions. As therapists, we do ourselves and our patients no service if we expect that we can—or ought to—provide all nuances of therapy equally well. No one can do everything, but we can all do a few things well. We can find other therapists who can perform competently in areas of specialization different from our own, and we can refer to them as needed.

Friendship

Adults from narcissistic families are often lonely people. Even if they are frenetically busy "doing" with groups of people, they frequently have no close friends, and they may have special difficulty with same-sex friendships. Remember Barbara (in Chapter Seven), the patient who was still in mourning and still feeling defective twenty years later because she did not have the kind of friendships portrayed in a movie? Part of her sorrow was based on the fantasy that "everyone else" had several intimate friends with whom they could share all their innermost feelings. It was a revelation for her to learn that many people felt as she did, and that in fact it was closer to the norm for people to be fortunate enough to have even one very close friend, and then a small circle of less intimate friends with whom one shared time and activities, but not one's "darker" or more vulnerable self. This is even more true for men, who commonly have only activity-specific (golfing buddies, poker "with the guys") or work-specific friendships. Even with fairly close friends, it is unusual to find intimacy among male friends. It is more usual for men to have a female friend with whom they can share intimacy than to have such a relationship with another male.

It is a sad, stupid, and unnecessary fact of life in our society that regardless of how bad things are, women often have each other; men are often alone. In our culture, the male myth sets men up for isolation: if real men do not eat quiche, then they certainly do not start sentences with "I feel." When women are trying to learn to trust and to reach out for sharing relationships, they are likely to be able to link up with other healthy, sharing women. If men try the same thing, they are likely to experience rejection from men who are frightened of intimacy. In this homophobic society, men who would like to have the freedom to discuss their feelings and would like to have intimate friendships with other men are often regarded with suspicion, out of fear that intimacy may lead to a sexual relationship. Perhaps that is why these men may seek out female friends; of course, these relationships can be problematic for the same reason. In our society, intimacy and sexuality are closely linked.

While there is a sexual component to all relationships, female/female friendships seem to have fewer problems in this area than do male/male friendships. It is common to see women friends embrace on meeting or saying good-bye; one has to do some heavy-duty looking to see the same thing between males.

If there is not a sexual conflict in female/female friendships, however, there is often a competitive conflict. Society contributes to this female/female conflict by limiting opportunities for women. There are just fewer career and leadership opportunities for women, so there is more competition for the opportunities that exist. For adult children of narcissistic homes, however, there is an added dimension. When one is not raised in an atmosphere of acceptance and unconditional love, one is likely to believe that a friend will only like you if you meet her needs. Because they have been brought up to know how difficult it is to meet other's needs, and how painful the rejection if one fails, it is not surprising that these individuals often sabotage friendships.

Too demanding, too accepting, too giving, too withholding, too manipulative, too erratic, too intrusive, too absent, too responsible, too irresponsible—these are some of the ways in which survivors "do in" their friendships. Essentially it is a spurious attempt at control, similar to the way the child attempts to take control in the narcissistic family. It is the "since you're going to reject me anyway, I'll bring it about myself" kind of destructive control that is learned by those who fear (or know) that they have no genuine control.

Relationships

Individuals who attempt to form relationships with these individuals often feel that they cannot "get in" emotionally. The message is often "I want you to come in—but not too far" or "only sometimes, and you have to guess when it's okay with me and when it's not!" Conversely, these individuals may become intimate very fast, only to become frightened of the intimacy and abruptly pull away. They want the intimacy—crave it, in fact—but become fearful that (1) they cannot sustain a relationship because of their defectiveness, (2) the other person will make demands that they are unwilling/unable to meet, or (3) the other person will find out how defective they are and reject them.

The solution to the discomfort of uncontrolled intimacy, therefore, is usually an attempt to control the *degree of intimacy*, often dooming the relationship to failure. Being a little bit intimate is like being a little bit pregnant; it does not happen in the real world. The relationship becomes a self-fulfilling prophesy: the individual knows it will fail and thus acts in ways to ensure that outcome. Either the significant other ultimately gives up because of the inequality of the relationship, or the survivor acts out on her feelings of fear and out-of-controlness by ending the relationship herself (the "I'll get you before you can get me" school of coping techniques).

As mentioned above, the institution of spurious control mechanisms is one of the lessons taught in narcissistic homes. Obviously, individuals who have been the "other half" of these relationships often feel used and hurt, victims of an abrupt rejection they cannot understand.

Both Ends of the Spectrum at Once

The strange juxtaposition of both ends of the spectrum being present simultaneously for any given personality trait is a common factor in adults raised in narcissistic homes.[2] (See Chapter Three for a discussion of characteralogic dualities represented in the Narcissus myth.) One of the interesting things that happens in group therapy with the survivors of narcissistic families is that persons will, usually for the first time, recognize that they themselves demonstrate both extremes of a particular trait when they hear those traits discussed by other group members.

Jean: "I don't trust anyone. I realize that a big part of my problem with men is that I hold them at arm's length. Eventually, they just say 'to hell with it' and move on to someone more responsive."

Sarah: *(nods vigorously)* "That's me, to a 'T.'"

Lizzie: "Sometimes I think I do that, but there are other times I just sort of bare my soul to anyone. You know—meet a guy at a party, tell him the story of my life, and go to bed with him. Slam, bang!"

Sarah: *(nods vigorously)* "That's me, too!"

The Plastic Wall

The concept of the erection of psychological barriers (or walls) as a defense against intimacy and the possibility of feeling pain has been well documented and described in the literature. (Perhaps the most succinct and helpful illustration of this concept is found in Eliana Gil's *Outgrowing the Pain*.[3] Of course, the inherent problem with psychological walls is the same as that of real walls: they keep out, but they may also trap within. As Frost put it:

> Before I built a wall I'd ask to know
> What I was walling in or walling out
> And to whom I was like to give offense.
> Something there is that doesn't love a wall,
> That wants it down.[4]

But many survivors *do* love their walls, and do not want them down. The high-functioning survivor of a narcissistic family may appear to have let the walls down, to be emotionally available in an appropriate way. And for all intents and purposes, he may be—most of the time. When he is feeling threatened, however, he detaches, becoming aloof, cool, and distant. Significant others can suddenly feel cut off. They become frightened, fearful of losing their loved one or parent; they feel guilty and responsible.

The adults who manifest the "plastic wall" (visualize someone wrapped in Saran Wrap—it is not very dense, but it is definitely protective) are often the products of covertly narcissistic families: they can be seen and touched and may do all the right things, but in times of extreme stress, there is an element of emotionality missing. These are the individuals whose significant others quickly learn not to push too far: not out of fear of provoking physical violence, but out of fear of their cold rejection. The more threatened these persons feel, the more intellectual, cold, quiet, withdrawn, and detached they become. Intellectualization is their coping mechanism of choice.

We use the term *plastic wall*, rather than *wall*, to differentiate degrees of emotional isolation. The survivor of traumatic abuse may be totally isolated emotionally. All therapists have worked with individuals who allow themselves to feel virtually nothing and allow no one to get close to them emotionally; much of Chapter Eight is about that kind of patient. But the plastic-wall survivor is different. These individuals really have "broken through" their walls and are able to share loving, close relationships. They make good parents, spouses, lovers, and best friends—until something happens. Usually it is a combination of stressors, the reintroduction of the original stressor, or the threatening of a well-established coping mechanism. For instance, when the individual's significant other complains about her working too many hours (her defense against feeling incompetent) or drinking too much wine at the party (her way of letting go of stress) or going to bed too late to make love (her way of dealing with feelings of personal unattractiveness), the plastic wall may go up.

The plastic wall rarely surfaces in individual counseling, as it is usually only seen by the intimate other. A way it may manifest itself in individual therapy, however, is when the patient can talk about feelings using the appropriate words, ("I felt hurt" or "I felt angry," for example), but with little or no corresponding affect. The patient knows what he feels, but he is protecting himself from experiencing those feelings. If he is like this in therapy, he is probably like this with his significant others. As we mentioned previously, the plastic-wall phenomenon is more of a consideration for therapists who are doing relationship counseling with adults from Narcissistic Families of origin. Because the plastic-wall phenomenon usually occurs in high-functioning people, in an atmosphere of support and caring it can quite easily be let down.

As something of a footnote, we also see this behavior frequently in military and quasi-military personnel. Because our Newport, Rhode Island, practice is close to the Naval War College, a relatively high percentage of our patients are in the U.S. Navy, U.S. Coast

Guard, or National Guard. They use the plastic wall at work as an effective and appropriate coping mechanism. When they come home, however, the behavior remains the same, even though it is no longer appropriate.

> **Amy and Jack's Story.** Amy and Jack were referred for marital counseling through their military family program. One of their major problems was the frequency of fights— almost every evening when they arrived home from work (she was a nutritionist in a doctor's office, he was a noncommissioned officer with the Coast Guard.) She said that while he could be the sweetest, most empathic man in the world, about half of the time she could not talk to him: "He won't listen to my feelings. He acts like our house is a courtroom and he's the prosecuting attorney! I have to prove—back up—everything I say! He acts so cold and imperious; I feel like he's just waiting for me to make a mistake so he can pounce on me and prove me wrong!"
>
> Jack was a high-functioning individual who had worked out his narcissistic family-of-origin issues in prior therapy. He still clung to the plastic wall as his behavior of choice in stressful situations, however. It worked very well in the military; it just did not work at home. One of the first changes the couple agreed to initiate had to do with re-entry behavior: when they got home from work, they would have minimal contact until Jack had showered and put on civilian clothes. Getting out of the uniform was a signal to him that he was not "Chief"—he was Jack, husband of Amy. The fights essentially stopped, and they both learned to recognize and deal with this behavior effectively.

Conclusion

Until survivors are able to work through their multiple issues (trust, responsibility and control, boundary setting, and the like), they will have difficulty in establishing and maintaining an intimate relationship. If they are in a dysfunctional relationship of some duration, they may also be reluctant to commit fully to therapy out of fear that they will lose the relationship if they get better. The less they get from the relationship, the more they may fight to save it (remember, the less you have, the more valuable it becomes). It is important to stress with these patients that the skills and character traits that will enable them to leave a relationship, confident in their ability to have a good life on their own, are the same skills and traits that will maximize their chances of making a relationship work. Even if they did not learn those skills in their family of origin, they can learn them now.

10
"I Do, Therefore I Am"
Versus Validating the Treasure

Task Competency: I Do, Therefore I Am

A major stumbling block faced by many individuals who are the products of narcissistic families is their overwhelming need for external validation. Often these individuals are able to compensate for this need by involving themselves in work situations where they are likely to receive some form of validation. For instance, journalists will see their words in print, nursery school teachers will get hugs and kisses for their work, clergypersons will have an audience on Sunday mornings, university professors will have the adulation of worshipful students, and therapists and physicians will see their words treated as gospel and acted on obediently by patients.

This ability to achieve validation through task competency is one of the ways in which these individuals get by in our society. These individuals are often successful "professional achievers," and very few onlookers would guess at their woeful lack of self-esteem. Their task competency, however, is both a blessing and a curse. On the one hand, the lawyer who is a hero to his clients gets many of his esteem needs met at work; on the other hand, if he attempts to disclose his need for validation to people close to him, he may be met with disbelief—or, worse, resentment and rejection. Very often, when successful survivors ask for help, they are met with a "What have you got to complain about?" attitude.

Further, if task competency is the only way an individual knows to prove to herself and to others that she has worth, then she must, by definition, have tasks to do. Thus there must always be more courses to take, more academic degrees to achieve, more jobs to volunteer for, more Little League teams to coach, more cookies to bake, more customers to sign, higher quotas to set, more souls to save, and on and on. The roots of workaholism are truly sown in narcissistic homes; "I do, therefore I am" could be the motto of many adult children from these homes.

Obviously, this need for external validation as a compensation for low self-esteem can cause problems in the workplace. The arena in which it is more commonly a problem, however, is in that of interpersonal relationships. Few of us marry cheerleaders, and yet the spouse of a narcissistic family survivor may often feel as if that is the expectation for his or her role. The survivor has great difficulty in any situation in which he is not given total approval and support. This can be an onerous burden for the spouse, significant other, or child of the individual, for as much as we may love or approve of another human being, we rarely approve totally of all of his actions, words, or ideas. This is doubly complex, as the person may have trouble discriminating between criticism (lack of approval) of her actions and criticism of her being. The corollary of "I do, therefore I am" is "Disapprove of what I do, disapprove of me."

The tendency to generalize lack of approval of specific behaviors (words, ideas, and so forth) to lack of approval of oneself as a human being is one of the more problematic areas for these individuals. Their worldview makes the very concept of constructive criticism a contradiction in terms. If disapproving of anything I do is disapproving of me, then there can be nothing "constructive" about it; *correction is rejection.* The employer or supervisor of this individual can find correction at work a nightmare, while the employee finds himself virtually destroyed by even the most kindly suggestion.

Conversely, the adult child raised in a narcissistic family may have trouble being a good employer, manager, or administrator, because she also equates correction with rejection and may have great difficulty in doing needed correction or discipline with staff. She may be unable to appropriately use the power inherent in her position.

Power and Responsibility

In Chapter Four we introduced the dyad of responsibility and control. The dyad of power and responsibility is also problematic for individuals from narcissistic homes. As these individuals are likely to assume responsibility for things they do not control, but refuse to assume responsibility for things they do control, so they also tend to exercise power they do not have and refuse to exercise the power they do have.

The problematic overuse of power has to do primarily with the all-or-nothing syndrome (see Chapter Six). For example, if one is put in charge of a committee, he may assumes that he has "all" the power and ride roughshod over the committee members (with unnecessary meetings, late-night phone calls, excessive reports, and so forth) so that "the job gets done right." The translation of this is that the chairperson has little confidence in himself or in anyone else and so overcompensates by using his power intrusively. He does not have the confidence to delegate authority and jobs, so he oversees and second-guesses everyone until they are miserable (the "all" part); then, when the committee members either complain, resign, or revolt, he throws up his hands and quits, or retreats and refuses to be in a leadership position at all (the "nothing" part).

What is more common for adults raised in narcissistic families, however, is the underuse of power. These individuals have a hard time with the concept that to underuse or refuse to use the power that one legitimately has is *also* to abuse that power. Narcissistic survivors are particularly susceptible to this condition because (1) their task-oriented world view (I do, therefore I am) makes them good workers, likely to achieve success in their field of endeavor, and (2) their low self-esteem and lack of essential trust make it difficult for them to accept the reality of their powerfulness. One cannot use power that one does not know—or refuses to accept—one has. But to refuse to recognize one's power is also inherently to abuse it.

The difficulty to accept and use power appropriately can run deep in these individuals. Since they have been well trained in their narcissistic families of origin to be reflective and reactive, they tend to be people pleasers. This need for acceptance frequently masks itself as a sort of hyperdemocracy: I cannot make a decision (or issue a judgment, or cut off discussion) because I must be fair to everyone.

Translation: I am afraid someone will not approve of me. This indecisiveness masquerading as "fairness" is abuse of power, and it is
sensed and resented by those whom it affects. Power carries on its
back responsibility; the willingness to use the power appropriately
and the integrity to stand behind the ultimate decisions that power
implies are what this responsibility is all about. Failure to follow
through in either area is abusive to those dependent on the one with
the power.

For instance, let us go back to the committee described above.
This time, however, the chairperson is a nice guy. He wants to make
sure that everyone gets to have his say, that all decisions are popular,
and that everyone feels good. The meetings last interminably,
because he refuses to limit discussion; there can never be decisions,
because everybody does not agree; and the meetings are horren-
dous, because the members with an axe to grind dominate the pro-
ceedings. The chairperson is refusing to use his power, and everyone
feels the abusive effects. Then, when the committee members either
complain, resign, or revolt, he throws up his hands . . . Sound familiar? The underuse of power ends up feeling the same for these individuals as the overuse of power did: they feel like they just cannot
get it right.

The Reality of the Now

The trick, of course, is the acceptance of the reality of the now. Just
as in accepting the reality of the past (see Chapter Four), these
patients need help to accept the reality of who they are now as
adults. Since the old tapes from the past keep replaying, urging them
not to overreach themselves or "get too big for their britches" (saying, "You're being selfish" or, "Who do you think you are?"), these
patients indeed need a reality check on *who they think they are*, to
reorient themselves as to their adult power and responsibility—otherwise known as their treasure.

The Treasure

The orientation we have found to be most helpful to patients in
dealing with the reality of the now, acceptance of power and respon-

sibility, and the fear of rejection that drives "people pleasing" is one that we call "the treasure." It is essentially the patient's recognition that what she *has* (in terms of character, talents, and traits)—what she *is*—is a treasure. It is unique to her alone, and it has value.

We ask patients to name their favorite color and their favorite gemstone. One patient answered "lavender" to color and "sapphire" to gemstone. I then told her to think of herself as a lavender sapphire; it is far rarer that a blue sapphire, and therefore far more valuable. But we noted that there was also the possibility that, because it is so unusual, many people would not recognize it as a sapphire. They might think it was an amethyst—pretty, but not too valuable. I asked the patient if that would affect the value of the stone; the answer, of course, was no. The inherent value of the stone remains the same whether or not someone knows what it is.

We go on to tell the patient that some people may not like the stone; they may throw it in the trash, or use it in their fishbowl for color. Does that affect the value of the stone? The answer is no again. Similarly, some people may say, "Ooh! A lavender sapphire! How ugly! Everybody knows that sapphires are supposed to be blue! In our family, we only do blue sapphires. You are different, and different is bad." But does that affect the intrinsic value of the treasure? We further explore the possibilities for the misidentification, undervaluing, and rejection of the stone. Each time we conclude that the value of the stone—of the treasure—is not dependent on others' recognition; it has intrinsic, genuine, and great value.

When a patient can visualize herself as a treasure, (such as a lavender sapphire), she is able to look at herself and her relationships differently. She is instructed to keep this idea of her treasure in the forefront of her mind—to see herself as a lavender sapphire, yellow emerald, or whatever—all week, and to judge other's reactions to her in that perspective. For instance, if someone does not value her (her treasure) very highly, it might be because they are ignorant—they do not know about lavender sapphires. That is unfortunate, but it does not devalue the sapphire. There will be a few people who will recognize the value and appreciate the treasure; the trick is to find those people and not feel too disheartened by the others. If some of those others can be educated as to the value of lavender sapphires, that is great. But if some people will choose to remain in ignorance and to reject what they do not understand, that is simply too bad. To others, the value may be irrelevant, as they just do not like lavender sapphires. That is okay; however, it does not lessen the value of the stone.

When patients return the next week, they will usually start out by talking about their "lavender sapphire." They do not forget, and it affects the way they see themselves. They can then more readily understand their responsibility and power from this new perspective. They also have a new framework within which to process rejection. The concept of seeing oneself as a treasure is a powerful one for patients. When what one has—what one *is*—is a treasure, one feels and acts differently. One does not have to *do* anything to be valuable; the worldview of "I do, therefore I am" becomes irrelevant. The new motto might be *"I am, therefore I have value."*

Conclusion

According to therapists who have been trained in the use of the narcissistic family model, a particular strength of the model is in its ability to allow the patients to see their own family-of-origin experience in a way that makes them feel less "defectively special" (or, as one patient labeled it, less "terminally unique") and as more genuinely valuable; it is a positive, hopeful kind of therapy. These practitioners have felt empowered in their work by having a framework from which to operate—a model that adds techniques as well as structure and is appropriate with a large percentage of their patients.

Numerous patients have commented that it is refreshing and reassuring to have their therapist take a more active, directive role in their therapy. It makes them feel more confident of their therapist's ability to be a facilitator for positive change. It is reassuring for patients to know that their therapist has a goal for the therapy and can lead them through predictable stages on the way to that goal.

Appendix A: An Overview
of Narcissism in Psychoanalytic Theory

T o say that there have been volumes of material written on narcissism and psychoanalytic theory would hardly prepare the uninitiated for the seemingly endless array of essays, articles, books, and compendiums written over the last century on the subject. For the reader who wishes a review of the salient features of this topic, plus our annotations, we offer the following modest overview.

Narcissism as a Means of Resolving Conflict

Reducing Freud's theory of narcissism to its simplest, we are talking about conflict resolution: the child's ability to move from what Freud labels primary narcissism (identifying the mother as a primary love object) to the "normal" Oedipal phase.[1] Essentially, Freud describes narcissism in terms of object love:

A person may love:

1. According to the narcissistic type:
   a. what he himself is (i.e., himself)
   b. what he himself was

139

    c. what he himself would like to be

    d. someone who was once part of himself

2. According to the anaclitic (attachment) type:

    a. the woman who feeds him

    b. the man who protects him and the succession of substitutes who take their place.[2]

In Freudian terms, healthy object relationships are of the attachment or anaclitic type, while unhealthy ones are narcissistic. Further, primary narcissism, as in an infant—who knows no object other than the self, and who cannot differentiate between ego and id[3]—is a natural, transitory state. Secondary (or pathological) narcissism, conversely, occurs when the libido is withdrawn from external objects and reinvested in its own ego (the self).[4]

Freud's 1914 essay "On Narcissism," which we recommend for reading or rereading in its original form, is a short, well-formulated, beautifully written exposition. In it, Freud introduces his theories on primary and secondary narcissism, refines his model of object relations, and reinforces and extends libido theory. In the context of the late twentieth century, however, Freud's gender distinctions may give offense to some clinicians. For example, in discussing object choice in males within the framework of normal narcissistic libidinal development, Freud asserts, "Complete object-love of the attachment type is, properly speaking, characteristic of the male. It displays the marked sexual overvaluation which is doubtless derived from the child's original narcissism and thus corresponds to a transference of that narcissism to the sexual object."[5] In contrast, the discussion of female object choice reads, "Women, especially if they grow up with good looks, develop a certain self-contentment which compensates them for the social restrictions that are imposed upon them in their choice of object. Strictly speaking, it is only themselves that such women love with an intensity comparable to that of a man's love for them".[6]

Read almost one hundred years after they were written, these words sound incredibly sexist; if viewed from a historical perspective, however, the genius of Freud's work is not lost. Even Freud gave a quasi apologia in a later essay, assuring us that his statements regarding feminine erotic life did not reflect "any tendentious desire on my part to deprecate women. . . . There are quite a number of women who love according to the masculine type and who develop the sexual overvaluation proper to that type."[7] Not too convincing, perhaps, but demonstrative of good intentions.

In looking at the primary narcissism of children—again, within a normal, nonpathological context—Freud takes a leap from the child's narcissistic crisis in transferring object love (from self to others) to the parent's narcissistic crisis in raising the child: "Parental love, which is so moving and at bottom so childish, is nothing but the parents' narcissism born again, which, transformed into object love, unmistakably reveals its former nature."[8] In a somewhat simplistic framework, Freud speaks of all parents—and all developmental stages of parenting—as if they were alike. Of course, they are not. As children develop in stages, so do parents; as the child will, it is hoped, move out of the stage of primary narcissism, so will a healthy parent system "get a grip" on its identification with the child and not live vicariously through him. When they are not able to do this, a narcissistic family system may develop. From our perspective, there is a continuum of narcissism, as there is of parental skill. That is not to say that Freud's views on parental narcissism are completely misguided. We, however, see no commanding evidence that it is true for most parent systems; rather, it presents the worst-case scenario.

Freud's theory of what he called the "narcissistic neuroses," which was later expanded in numerous works, poignantly delineated the essential paradoxes buried beneath the narcissistic exterior. These paradoxes became the springboard of theories and treatises on the subject by Klein through Kohut: grandiosity masking insecurity, egocentrism masking low self-esteem, and self-hate masquerading as self-love.[9] Later theorists sought to describe and explain additional paradoxes: cool indifference shattered by episodes of narcissistic rage;[10] the creation of the false self to hide and protect the vulnerable and unworthy true self,[11] and the inability to embrace empathic responses when empathy is the therapeutic key to unlocking and freeing the narcissistic personality.[12] While delivering what most scholars would consider to be the seminal work on narcissism, Freud also delivers a caution to therapists: "In the narcissistic neuroses the resistance is unconquerable; at the most, we are able to cast an inquisitive glance over the top of the wall and spy out what is going on on the other side of it."[13]

It is a far stretch from Freud's hypothesis to the DSM-III-R definition of narcissism as a personality disorder. Along the way, there have been many interpreters and refiners of Freud's theories, along with those whose theories diverge from Freud's. The most notable perhaps is Kohut, who contributed to the understanding of the psychology of the self and postulated about the role empathy plays in symptom formation in childhood and symptom resolution in therapy.[14] Although Freud's work on narcissism was by no means his most well-researched or documented effort, it is the basis of all other theories on narcissism.

Contemporary Literature: The British School, Mahler, Kernberg, Kohut, and Others

The post-Freudian period has spawned numerous adherents of Freudian perspective, most notably the object-relations school. This British influence is epitomized by the work of Melanie Klein, W.R.D. Fairbairn, Harry Guntrip, and D. W. Winnicott.[15] Margaret Mahler has emerged as the preeminent object-relations theorist in the United States.[16]

Klein

Klein's object-relations theory, in essence, discusses the relationship between the mother and infant within the first year of life. The first "object"—entity separate from itself, either existing as a discrete, viable entity or as an internalized mental representation—with whom the infant has a relationship may be, for instance, the mother's breast. The ability of the infant to organize itself around the relationship to the mother as an external love object is a prerequisite to healthy ego development.

Mahler

Mahler has described the process of healthy ego development in voluminous writings; a brief review of this process follows:

1. The "normal autism phase"[17] (or Freud's primary narcissism[18]), in which the child is merged with the mother.

2. The "symbiotic phase," in which the infant becomes aware both of his own ability to achieve pleasure (lack of tension, as in sneezing and defecating) as well as to get pleasure from his mother (feeding, cuddling). He begins to recognize outside stimuli (objects) and strives for achievement of homeostasis. This is the beginning of the separation-individuation process.[19]

3. The stage at which narcissism is most likely to form, in object-relations theory, is the crossroads labeled the rapprochement crisis.[20] If at this point the child is empathically encouraged in both of her contrasting needs for autonomy from and for fusion with her mother, she will pass through this stage and move into the next phase, the Oedipal phase.[21] For us, the push-pull of this phase is best represented by the toddler's early attempts at walking; she takes a few steps, looks back to see that the mother is still there, takes a few more steps, and then must run back to the safety of the mother's arms. In cases where the mother will not let go—or, conversely, where the mother will not welcome back—the seeds of narcissism are sown. (See also Sophie Freud's work on overloving/underloving, a symptom of the narcissistic family[22].)

Kernberg

The most notable student of object-relations theory with regard to the psychoanalytic study of narcissism is Otto Kernberg, professor of psychiatry at Cornell University and author of the classic *Borderline Conditions and Pathological Narcissism*.[23] Kernberg classifies the narcissistic personality as a subgroup of borderline disorder. He differentiates normal narcissism, which does not impair the ability for object relationships, from pathological narcissism, which is seen as a serious deterioration in this capacity. He characterizes narcissists as excessively self-absorbed, intensely ambitious, lacking in empathy, grandiose, having an inordinate need for praise and tribute from others, and unconcerned with the comfort of others except on the most superficial level. They experience pleasure only in the presence of admiration, and they become quickly bored in its absence.

Kernberg stresses the paradoxical dualities mentioned above (grandiosity/insecurity, and so on). He differentiates narcissistic from borderline personality disorder by the narcissistic personality's "having a cohesive, albeit highly pathological, grandiose self, which hides the inner identity diffusion and aimlessness.[24] Although it was Kohut who coined the term *narcissistic rage*, Kernberg describes a type of rage that is revengeful and compulsive; a driving need to "pay back" another for some insult or slight that threatens the narcissist's well-defended persona.[25]

Kernberg described three levels of narcissism. The first, who resemble Bach's "darlings of the gods,"[26] are successful or gifted enough that they manage to receive all the admiration they require, and so they may never enter therapy. The second are marginally successful but often seek treatment because of difficulty in maintaining long-term relationships or general feelings of aimlessness and dissatisfaction. The third group are those who are probably diagnosed with borderline personality disorder; they function clearly on a borderline level and manifest severe problems in the areas of impulse control, anxiety tolerance, and sublimation.[27] These narcissists also evidence paranoid traits (masked by haughtiness or detachment), believing others to be always lurking, waiting for opportunities to persecute them.[28]

While Kernberg is clearly a classical Freudian and tends to use medical terms (such as *malignant* and *terminal*) that cannot help but convey the severity—if not hopelessness—of the narcissistic condition, his exposition on what the narcissist faces in middle age (what the layperson would dub a "midlife crisis") is compassionate and empathic. To quote only a small portion: "[Because of] the gradual painful awareness that the narcissistic gratifications of youth and past triumphs are no longer available, and in order to avoid painful envy of his own past, the narcissistic patient is forced to devalue his own past achievements and accomplishments."[29] (Note the contrast of this with Kohut's perspective on narcissistic middle age, which is described below.)

Kernberg asserts often that the underlying aggressive qualities of the pathological narcissist, combined with his envy and need to control, make him a difficult patient. While Kernberg believes that analysis can be of value to pathological narcissists, he nonetheless states that the transference difficulties are extreme and present serious problems for the therapist. This is because of the narcissist's difficulty in seeing the therapist as a discrete being, independent of the narcissist, and his corresponding need to devalue both the skills of the therapist, and the nature of the therapy experience.[30]

Kohut

While Kernberg and others adhere to the Freudian psychoanalytic model, Heinz Kohut advocates an open-mindedness in terms of modality efficacy, including short-term, intensive psychotherapy.[31] Kohut was a professorial lecturer in the department of psychiatry at the University of Chicago, a faculty member and training analyst at the Chicago Institute for psychoanalysis, and visiting professor of psychoanalysis at the University of Cincinnati. As the reader will see below, in many ways he has been a maverick within the psychoanalytic/psychiatric community.

In sharp contrast to Kernberg, Kohut does not view narcissism as malignant or terminal; in fact, he does not even see pathological narcissism as a separate entity from primary narcissism, but rather as an developmental arresting or fixation of the primitive self. Kohut asserts that much of the judgmental and pejorative descriptive language of narcissistic personality disorder in DSM-III-R has more to do with a societal problem of skewed values than with the disorder itself. Indeed he is not too far from sympathy with Jung, who deplores the "impoverishment of symbolism" and urges a return to spirituality and true individuation of the self (in "Archetypes of the Unconscious"), or Fromm, who states that "the problem with our culture is not that there is too much selfishness, but too little genuine self-love."[32]

Kohut's first book, *Analysis of the Self*, set forth his theory of self psychology. In short, the child's narcissistic bliss is necessarily cut short by the child's own development and the mother's decreasing availability to meet his every need. Therefore, the child attempts to hold on to this narcissistic bliss by assigning to it (1) a grandiose and exhibitionistic image (the narcissistic self), and (2) an imagined, idealized parent imago—the completely devoted, all-powerful fantasy parent.[33]

If all goes well, the grandiose and exhibitionistic self will become tamed (socialized) and integrated over time into the adult personality capable of meeting its ego-syntonic needs and accomplishing its purposes. Further, if all goes well, the idealized parent imago becomes integrated into the adult personality in the form of values and ideals. If, however, the child suffers some narcissistic trauma, the grandiose self never becomes integrated, instead perpetuating itself and striving for its primitive-level fulfillment, which Kohut describes as "failure of the archaic selfobject."[34] Similarly, if a child suffers phase-inappropriate disappointments from the caretaking parent, the idealized parent imago is also retained intact, and the adult must search ceaselessly for a primitive transitional object to cling to for support, safety, and validation.[35]

Kohut's transference model, then, becomes easily understandable as the therapist allows the patient to cast him or her in the role of idealized parent imago. Whereas lack of parental empathy and/or consistency caused the narcissistic crisis, the transference can reestablish the imagined, idealized archaic parent imago for the patient, who can then resume the development process (idealizing transference). Likewise, if the therapeutic process requires a return to the archaic, grandiose self, the patient may cast the therapist in the role of self-object, or someone who exists in order to reflect back at the patient his or her accomplishments (mirroring transference).

Kohut was also responsible for the reporting of narcissistic rage, which develops out of a profound sense of disappointment and loss of self-objects. Much of Kohut's writing dealt with the analysis of narcissistic rage and its sociopolitical impact (he uses the theory to explain the rise of Hitler in Germany, to give but one example).[36]

While Kohut, like Kernberg, recognizes that the onset of middle age presents painful difficulties for the narcissist, particularly vis-à-vis the Jungian[37] concept of empty depression based on the "depleted self,"[38] he also believes that this time of life has possibilities for the transformation of narcissism and the finding of acceptance with life as it now is. For Kohut, "a certain inner peace results in middle age."[39]

Other Theorists and DSM-III-R

There are a number of other theorists who have made significant contributions to the field of knowledge. Bach documents cognitive peculiarities associated with narcissistic personality disorder.[40] Language, for example, takes on a different meaning: instead of clear communication of feelings, thoughts, or ideas, it is used in an auto-centric manner for regulating and enhancing self-esteem. Similarly, time loses its impersonal, abstract quality and is instead calculated by its internal, personal impact. Bach also comments on the presence of mood swings in narcissism, as moods are excessively dependent on external stimuli, reinforcement, or lack of same.[41]

Cooper[42] has linked narcissism with masochistic tendencies, as have Stolorow and Lachmann,[43] and even Kohut in a short (inconclusive) discussion of Dr. Neiderland's case of homosexual masochistic perversion,[44] whereas Bach,[45] Baumeister,[46] Freud,[47] and numerous others have linked narcissistic pathology with sadism.

While the definitions, clinical descriptions, and treatment constructs for dealing with narcissistic personality disorder are numerous, for clinical practitioners looking for third-party reimbursement, all of the above are delineated in the DSM-III-R.[48] 301.81 is the DSM-III-R coding for narcissistic personality disorder. The essential feature is a personality disorder characterized by the above noted characteristics of grandiosity, exaggerated sense of self-importance, exhibitionistic need for attention and approval, fantasies of success, cool indifference or marked feelings of rage in reaction to perceived threats to self-esteem, disturbances in interpersonal relationships, lack of empathy. There is no information available on such predisposing factors as sex and family patterns, while the differential diagnosis lists borderline and histrionic personality disorders. Some therapists, however, assert that there exists a bias toward designating these disorders as more characteristically female.

Conclusion

To paraphrase Chessick, narcissism has a wide range of meanings.[49] Theories of narcissism have developed along a continuum ranging from normal (essential) narcissism to narcissistic personality disorder (pathological). The above synopsis highlights the more salient features of psychoanalytic theory relating to the development of the concept of the narcissistic family.

Appendix B: Therapy with the Blakes

The following case vignette is actually a combination of two therapy sessions with one couple, the Blakes. This particular case was chosen because the transcripts of these two sessions touched on so many topics covered in the narcissistic family treatment model, in terms of both subject matter explored and therapy techniques used.

Session one was involved primarily with helping the Blakes to "narrow the focus" (to combat the tendency toward generalization) in their discussions by concentrating on their communication style— setting up "fair fighting rules" and creating an atmosphere wherein the central issues could be discussed in safety. In session two, the Blakes were then able to attack the narcissistic family-of-origin issues forming the core of their communication problems.

In the telling of this case story, where narcissistic family issues or concepts—such as mind reading, "I do, therefore I am," setting boundaries, and owning feelings—are discussed, they are noted by { }, as in {owning feelings}. Where illustrations of specific therapeutic techniques are used, especially in session two, they are noted in [ ], as in [clarification].

Except for editing to preserve patient confidentiality, the abridged text of these two sessions appears as it occurred.

The Blakes' Story

At the end of her therapy (to be terminated because of her husband's job transfer), Mrs. Blake called to ask if her husband could come with her to a therapy session.

Mrs. Blake was an incest survivor who had been in therapy for eighteen months. Although she had made great strides in therapy, she was apprehensive about the interruption of her treatment and the need to find another therapist after the move. Since Mr. Blake had come in with his wife from time to time to deal with specific issues vis-à-vis the effects of the incest on his wife's ability to relate to him sexually, he felt comfortable with the therapist, and no major comfort, safety, or therapeutic allegiance issues needed to be addressed.

Session One

When they arrived, the Blakes were agitated. They tried to chitchat for a few moments, but it was obvious that they had an agenda and that they found it to be mildly embarrassing. After a few looks and nudges, Mr. Blake said, "You've got to help us to communicate better. We're at each other's throats all the time. We can't say two words to each other without it ending up a huge fight." Mrs. Blake nodded assent. "With the pressure of the move and everything, it seems that any progress we've made is shot. I just feel so angry with him all the time!"

"Oh, it's not just her," Mr. Blake jumped in, ever protective. "We've both been angry and losing our tempers a lot." At this point, it was apparent that the Blakes were getting uncomfortable. Mrs. Blake quickly became defensive at any hint of criticism, and Mr. Blake always rushed to her defense—even in the absence of attack. As the scenario unfolded, it was revealed that the tension in the house was causing constant friction between the Blakes, and they were unable to resolve one conflict without another immediately taking its place. The Blakes were lost; they knew that they were treating each other unkindly and unfairly, but they both felt under attack and angry most of the time.

The therapist felt that concrete rules would be helpful here [narrowing the focus], the kind of list that one can take home and put on the refrigerator door. Many patients find specific suggestions helpful to defuse anxiety temporarily. Because they have the safety of the list, they are then able to relax and talk about deeper issues. The therapist listed the following impediments to fair fighting on the board {list making; adapted from Block's *The Intimate Enemy*[1]}:

- "You" messages—accusatory statements
- Name calling—"lazy slob," "lying bitch," and so on
- Family references—"You're just like your mother!" (or father, lazy brother)
- Gunnysacking—storing up grievances and then trotting them out during a fight
- Historical references—"You did the same thing the last time my friends were here!" (or last New Year's, or ten years ago)
- "Always" and "never"—"You never help with the children; I always have to do everything myself!"

The therapist explained that these are techniques that people commonly use during fights, and that they are counterproductive. If the purpose of the fight is to air strong feelings that may be oppositional and come to a resolution, then it is important to stay on the topic, keep the focus narrow, and avoid all the above stratagems. They are hurtful, widen the focus, and will preclude the possibility of resolution.

The Blakes laughed knowingly at the list—and wrote it down. Individually, they went through the list and noted their own special favorites. Mr. Blake favored "you" messages and historical references; Mrs. Blake liked "you" messages, name calling, and gunnysacking. Neither of them used family references, but they both confessed to using historical references and "always/never" on occasion. They both indicated that they thought the list was helpful, and that they might be able to begin to recognize those destructive stratagems in themselves and each other.

This was not the end of the problem for the Blakes. Actually, it did not even address the real problem. But because it was *related* to the problem but not the problem itself, the patients did not feel threatened. They felt that they had learned something useful, that they had something concrete to take away with them (the list), and that they had been validated—if there is a list, then other people do the same things, and they are not alone (that is, uniquely deficient, lacking, stupid, bad). The introduction of the list narrowed the focus for the Blakes; they were able to relax, laugh a bit, and start to see their situation as a problem to be solved rather than as a condition of being. They did not think that their problems were now solved, but they did have a feeling that their problems might be able to be dealt with incrementally—in pieces—and thus become more manageable.

Session Two

Two days later, the Blakes returned. They reported that their verbal interactions had improved because they were using the list, but that their level of anger and frustration was still very high. Mrs. Blake returned to the subject of her extreme anger at her husband. "I just about can't stand to talk to him at all—about anything! He makes me so mad all the time!"

"She does seem mad at me a lot," Mr. Blake volunteered sadly, then hastened to add, "but we've been short with each other, it's not just her." Looking as if she might explode, Mrs. Blake corrected, "I'm not talking about you, John, I'm talking about me—about how I feel. And most of the time you just ignore me and don't seem to give a damn about my feelings!" Seeing the session about to go down the tubes, the therapist asked Mrs. Blake for one example of a recent time when her husband appeared not to care about her feelings and she had become angry.

She had an example immediately: "My glasses! I needed new glasses, because I hadn't been seeing well for a long time now, and my old glasses were really hurting me on the nose; they were too heavy. Even if they hadn't been too heavy, I would've needed new ones; I needed bifocals. Anyway, I kept telling John that I needed to go and get my prescription changed and pick out new frames, but he could've cared less. Every time I'd suggest a time we could go, he'd have an excuse not to make the trip. Of course, let his truck need something, and he's making the twenty-five-mile trip to the dealer with no problem. So, anyway, I finally get him to take me, I pick out the glasses, and they make them up while we get a sandwich. We go back to pick them up, he sees the bill, and he goes crazy! I wanted to kill him! He says, 'You couldn't have found any cheaper frames?'

And, 'Did you really have to have 'em tinted,' real sarcastic like. He made me feel so small. Like I wasn't worth having nice glasses. I would've returned them, if I could have. He took all the joy out of it for me." Turning to look at him, she said tearfully, "I felt like you thought I was a piece of crap."

"Honey," Mr. Blake began. "If I could have ripped out my tongue, I would have. I was just shocked!" Turning to the therapist, he asked, "Wouldn't you be shocked if someone handed you a bill for three hundred dollars? For glasses?" Turning back to his wife, "I'm sorry that I overreacted. It was temporary. I'm glad you have the glasses. I know that you needed them. But I've told you that a hundred times. What more do you want from me?"

The therapist thanked them for their re-creation of the event and praised them for their willingness to discuss it [positive feedback]. "Tell me again, Pam, how you felt when John got angry." Mrs. Blake said, "I felt—small. Like I had overreached myself. Like—like I was worthless" {owning feelings}.

"What did you feel like John was really thinking and feeling?"

"I knew what he was feeling! He hated me. He thought that I wasn't worth that money. He thought I was a terrible, ugly person for buying what I wanted with his hard earned money—even though I said I'd pay for them. And I did. Pay for them. That's another thing. I gave him the money." {mind reading}.

The therapist raised her hand in a "time out" signal and said, "I know that there's more, but I want to stick to this one topic for now [narrowing the focus]. Okay?" Mrs. Blake nodded assent. The therapist turned to Mr. Blake, who looked acutely miserable. "Honestly," he started, "I never meant . . ."

Again, the therapist called for time out. "John, I'm going to ask you some questions, and I want you to answer them as honestly as you can. I know what you want to communicate, and we'll get there eventually, I promise. Now—honestly—did you want to go to the city to get Pam's glasses?"

Mr. Blake looked hesitantly at the therapist, then at his wife. "Well . . . I knew she needed the glasses—and of course I wanted her to have them!"

The therapist clarified: "But was it a priority with you? Was it something you jumped out of bed thinking about? Was it like, 'Oh, wow! Goody! Today I get to take Pam get her glasses! Oh, thank you, thank you, God!' " Both Blakes were laughing now [humor/hyperbole]. "No," Mr. Blake volunteered, smiling. "I certainly didn't feel like that! I really wasn't looking forward to the trip. I mean, I knew we'd have to get the glasses sooner or later, but I hate driving in all that traffic with the road construction and the tourists" {owning feelings}.

"I want to make sure I've got it right," the therapist said. "You knew at some level that you were going to have to go get the glasses, but it wasn't a major priority for you, and you weren't looking forward to the trip. Is that pretty accurate?" {clarification}.

"Yup, that's how I felt," Mr. Blake nodded.

"Then, when you got to the place, you had a snit over the amount of the bill, is that correct?"

"Well, yes," Mr. Blake agreed. "But only because it was so much money and I wasn't expecting it! It had nothing to do with . . ."

The therapist signaled another time out. "Did it bother you to spend three hundred dollars on eyeglasses?" she asked. "Yes," Mr. Blake answered {owning feelings}. "Well, I wasn't exactly overjoyed about it myself!" Pam jumped in.

The therapist nodded at her and smiled, but returned to Mr. Blake. "Let's see if I've got it. You knew she needed glasses, you weren't looking forward to the trip, and when you finally went, you had a fit at the amount of the bill. As far as it goes, is that accurate?"

"As far as it goes, yes," Mr. Blake agreed.

The therapist sat back, looking pleased. "I get it now. Obviously, you hate Pam and wish she were dead" [extension, hyperbole].

They both looked momentarily stunned. Then Mrs. Blake started to laugh, and Mr. Blake started to sputter. The therapist continued: "Hey—it's perfectly apparent to me. What else could he possibly have meant? He said he was mad about the cost of the glasses. But you knew that he really meant that he hated you! You could read his mind, isn't that right, Pam?" There was a glimmer of recognition, but Mrs. Blake was confused. "I'm not sure. I mean, I didn't really think he meant *that*!" she said.

"Didn't you?" the therapist queried. "Think back, Pam. Remember what it felt like when John expressed anger. Did you really believe he was just talking about the glasses? What did it feel like to you?" Mrs. Blake got teary and started to nod.

"When you were in the optical shop, and John got angry, did you feel like a grown, competent woman at that moment?"

Mrs. Blake shook her head, indicating "no."

"What did you feel like?" the therapist asked her.

"Like a little girl," she replied, wiping her eyes. "It's like, when he gets angry with me—when anyone gets angry with me—I feel like a little kid" {old tapes}.

"Did you feel like John disapproved of what you did, or of you? Did he hate the price of the glasses, or did he hate you?"

"I felt like . . ." She stopped and started to grin, then said, "Like he hated me and wished I were dead." She looked at the therapist. "It sounds ridiculous when I say it, because I know it's not true. But you're right. That's what it feels like at the time" {generalization, I do . . . I am}.

Mr. Blake leaned over and took her hand. "Honey," he said, "I never—honestly—felt like I . . ."

Mrs. Blake interrupted him. "John, I know that's not what you meant. Really. But that's what I feel at the time. It sounds ridiculous. But that's how I feel—at that moment."

The therapist then broke into their conversation. "Okay. This is great! Pam, John, you're on to something here. I want to go a little farther with this. Is that all right with you?" [positive feedback].

They both nodded enthusiastically. "Sure." "Go for it!"

The therapist leaned forward to Mr. Blake and said, "John-honestly, now—which would you rather do?" She leaned back, holding up one finger and talking like Arlo Guthrie [humor]. "Number one—take your truck into the shop, and hang out there with the guys talking about mufflers, and dual cam thingies, and all kinds of groovy truck stuff, *or*"—the therapist held up two fingers and smiled conspiratorially at Mrs. Blake, who was giggling—"drive thirty miles through heavy traffic to the city only to wait around for three hours for the privilege of paying three hundred dollars for a pair of glasses that you'll never even wear?" {reality checking}.

Mr. Blake was laughing now, too. "I plead guilty to number one."

"Aha!" the therapist said. "Just as I suspected!" Then she turned to Mrs. Blake, who was still smiling and patting her husband's hand. She leaned forward, beckoned Mrs. Blake toward her, and dropped her voice. "Pam, tell me the truth. Which would you rather do: Go to the jewelry store and try on two carat, emerald-cut diamond rings for two or eleven hours, or give your poor, tired husband a neck massage? Which would you rather do?" [hyperbole].

"You know me too well. I'd give him the massage if he really needed it, but . . ." She paused hesitantly.

"Which would you *rather* do—prefer to do, for you?" the therapist prompted.

"Well I'd much rather go to jewelry stores and try on diamonds. I'd rather do that than—than eat ice cream!" {owning feelings/preferences}.

"Does that mean, then, that you hate John? I mean, if you would prefer to go to a jewelry store than do something of interest to him—like work on the truck or shop for computers or give him a massage?" asked the therapist.

"No."

"Does it mean that some things are higher priority for you than they are for him?"

"Yes, I guess so."

"And is that unreasonable? I mean, are you a selfish witch if you like diamonds better than trucks? Or are you a normal person with natural preferences?"

"I'm not sure," Mrs. Blake responded. "I feel guilty if I want something different than he wants. I feel like he *thinks* I'm a selfish witch."

"So you can read his mind again. Let's save that for one minute. Pam, do you really believe that all people who are married should care equally about the same things? Do you honestly feel that you should like trucks?"

"No, I guess I don't. When I think about it, I guess it's okay for me to like some things he doesn't," Mrs. Blake volunteered.

"Wonderful. Let's go back to the glasses. Would you say that getting those glasses was a high priority for you? That you wanted them and needed them, and they were right here"—the therapist gestured at her forehead—"at the front of your mind a lot of the time?"

"Yes, definitely. I really needed them. It wasn't just vanity either . . ."

The therapist smiled at her, raising a hand to silence her. "We're talking about preferences and feelings. They exist all on their own; they don't need justification."

Mrs. Blake nodded.

"Okay. Here's a box." The therapist drew a small box in the air with her hands. "This box is labeled 'Pam's Glasses.' In here, we're going to put all of Pam's feelings and preferences about her glasses. Her feelings of need, her sense of urgency, her desire for lightweight frames and rose tinting, whatever. This is a box filled with all Pam's feelings and wishes about her glasses. Right?" The Blakes both nodded. "Now, Pam, take the box. It belongs to you." The therapist handed Mrs. Blake the "box." "You can put it on your lap." Mrs. Blake put it carefully on her lap. "Take care of it. It's precious to you. It has your feelings in it." Mrs. Blake smiled, and patted the "box" {compartmentalization } [boxes].

The therapist turned to Mr. Blake. "John, here's a box." She drew another "box" in the air. "This box is also labeled 'Pam's Glasses'— maybe this label is navy blue, and the other one was pink. Anyway, this box is going to be filled with all your feelings about Pam's glasses. That you want her to have them, that you dread the drive, that they're too expensive, whatever all those feelings are. We're putting them into the box. Now, here." The therapist handed him the box. "It's heavy," Mr. Blake commented. "I'll bet it is!" the therapist agreed {compartmentalization} [boxes].

"Now you each have your own boxes. Is that okay with you?" the therapist asked [clarification]. The Blakes nodded.

"John, are you comfortable with your box—or would you prefer to have hers?"

"Mine's fine," Mr. Blake said.

"Do you mind that she has one, too? That it's different from yours?" the therapist asked.

"No, she can have her own box. It doesn't bother me," he laughed.

"Great. Terrific. I love this! Pam, are you comfortable with your little package there? Is it okay for you?"

"Yeah, I like it. It's mine," Mrs. Blake said.

"He's got one, too. Is that a problem for you?"

"No. He's got his—I've got mine. It's fine. But he can't have mine," she added, with mock severity.

"Do you want his?" the therapist asked.

"No. I'll just keep mine, thank you," she replied.

"One last question, Pam. If John changes what's in his box— rearranges it, throws some stuff out, adds one or two things—does that affect your box? Does that mean that you have do something with your box, too? Change it, in any way?" [reality checking].

Mrs. Blake thought for a bit. "I don't think so. I mean, what's in my box is very personal. It might be affected, but I don't think it would. I mean, what I feel is what I feel. My feelings change, but that comes from in here"—she pointed to her head—"not out there. To answer your question, no."

"Okay, folks. What you have said is that you both have feelings, preferences, priorities. You own them. You have a right to them. They are personal. It is okay for your feelings about the same subject to differ. In other words, Pam can have one set of feelings about the glasses. John can have another set of feelings about the glasses. Furthermore, those feelings are in a box; they are limited, manageable. They aren't somehow cosmic, unlimited, spilling over into fifty other things—they are about one subject only. You can put them in a box. They are only about the glasses. They are not about Pam or her worth, or anything else. All other subjects have their own boxes. Do you agree with this? Does it feel right to you?" (clarification).

Both Blakes strongly agreed, and they liked the concept. After some discussion, the subject was brought back to the original topic. "Let's say that there's a full moon, or a solar eclipse, or some other weird happening and you forget all this stuff about boxes and feelings. It's just gone, wiped out. And—let's use you again, Pam—you have something that's just terribly important to you. Help me out here. What might it be?"

Mrs. Blake had one immediately: "This is a real one. Going to the china outlet. I desperately want new dishes before we leave here, and John thinks of twenty million reasons why we can't go. I feel hurt that he can't make the time; I really want to go!" {RAC}.

"That's perfect. So let's say that one day you pin him down on this, and he says that he can't go that day because . . . what?" The therapist looked at Mr. Blake.

He picked it up. "Because I'm really tired; work has been just plain hell lately, and I'd planned to take a day to just relax and putter around."

"How do you feel, Pam? Remember, you've forgotten all the good stuff we talked about today."

"I feel really hurt. He couldn't love me very much if he doesn't care about the dishes. I'm hurt and angry," Mrs. Blake said.

"He says that he's tired, but you can read his mind. You know that he means that—he hates you and wishes you were dead!" (They both start to laugh.) "Isn't that right?" The Blakes both nodded, and Mrs. Blake said, "Yes."

"What about if you just check it out? If, just to be absolutely sure that your mind-reading apparatus is functioning perfectly, you ask him if that's what he meant. Something like, 'You say that you don't want to go because you're really tired, but I think you mean that you hate me and wish I were dead. Is that what you mean?' Could you do that, Pam?" [reality checking].

"I could do that. I'd feel a little silly," she said.

"But you think it, don't you?" Mrs. Blake nodded. "And you act on those thoughts. So, why not check it out? Try it."

The Blakes finished the role play, in which Pam asked John if he hated her and wished her dead. Amidst some hilarity, he was able to clarify his feelings, and she was able to better express her feelings of urgency. John was able to indicate the times his schedule would permit a half day's absence from work {setting boundaries}, and they agreed to a day in the next week to make the trip.

Conclusion

Mrs. Blake was the survivor of an overtly narcissistic family. In this session a number of her family-of-origin issues surfaced, making respectful adult communication difficult. Mrs. Blake's family-of-origin experience, as noted earlier, was characterized by incest. But her issues and skill deficits were those shared by many adult children of narcissistic families.

References

Introduction

1. John Bradshaw, *Healing the Shame That Binds You* (Deerfield Beach, FL: Health Communications, 1988); Claudia Black, *It Will Never Happen to Me* (Denver, CO: MAC Printing and Publications, 1987); Eliana Gil, *Outgrowing the Pain* (New York: Dell, 1988); Janet G. Woititz, *Adult Children of Alcoholics*, expanded version (Deerfield Beach, FL: Health Communications, 1990).
2. Ellen Bass and Laura Davis, *The Courage to Heal: A Guide for Women Survivors of Child Sexual Abuse* (New York: Perennial Library, 1988); Steven Grubman-Black, *Broken Boys/Mending Men* (New York: Ivy Books, 1992).
3. Gil, op. cit.; Woititz, op. cit.
4. A. H. Maslow, *Toward a Psychology of Being* (New York: Van Nostrand, 1962); E. H. Erikson, *Identity: Youth and Crisis* (New York: W. W. Norton, 1968).
5. Hilde Bruche, *Learning Psychotherapy: Rationale and Ground Rules* (Cambridge, MA: Harvard University Press, 1974).
6. J. Wolpe, *The Practice of Behavioral Therapy*, 2nd ed. (New York: Paragon Press, 1973).
7. Jeffrey Berman, *Narcissism and the Novel* (New York: New York University Press, 1990), p. 26.

Chapter 1

1. Ovid, *Metamorphoses*, translated by Frank Justin Miller (1916; reprint, Cambridge, MA: Harvard University Press, 1936).
2. John Bradshaw, *Healing the Shame That Binds You* (Deerfield Beach, FL: Health Communications, 1988), p. 52.
3. Jacques Lacan, *The Seminar of Jacques Lacan*, edited by Alan Miller

and translated by John Forester, 2 vols. (Cambridge, UK: Cambridge University Press, 1988).

4. E. H. Erikson, *Identity: Youth and Crisis* (New York: W. W. Norton, 1968); A. H. Maslow, *Toward a Psychology of Being* (New York: Van Nostrand, 1962).

5. Terry Kellogg, *Finding Balance: 12 Priorities for Interdependence and Joyful Living* (Deerfield Beach, FL: Health Communications, 1991), p. 192.

Chapter 2

1. 20th Century-Fox Film Corporation, *The King and I*, remastered video recording (New York: CBS Fox Video, 1991).

2. E. H. Erikson, *Identity: Youth and Crisis* (New York: W. W. Norton, 1968); Margaret S. Mahler, Fred Pine, and Anni Bergman, *The Psychological Birth of the Human Infant* (New York: Basic Books, 1975).

3. Margaret S. Mahler, *On Human Symbiosis and the Vicissitudes of Individuation* (New York: International Universities Press, 1968).

4. Otto Kernberg, *Borderline Conditions and Pathological Narcissism* (New York: Jason Aronson, 1975).

5. Sigmund Freud, "On Narcissism: An Introduction," in *The Standard Edition of the Complete Psychological Works of Sigmund Freud*, vol. 14, edited and translated by James Strachey (1914; reprint, London: Hogarth Press, 1953–1974).

6. Ibid.

7. Marion F. Soloman, *Narcissism and Intimacy: Love and Marriage in an Age of Confusion* (New York: W. W. Norton, 1989).

Chapter 3

1. American Psychiatric Association, *Diagnostic and Statistical Manual of Mental Disorders*, revised 3rd ed. (Washington, DC: American Psychiatric Association, 1987).

2. Sigmund Freud, "On Narcissism: An Introduction," in *The Standard Edition of the Complete Psychological Works of Sigmund Freud*, vol. 14, edited and translated by James Strachey (1914; reprint, London: Hogarth Press, 1953–1974).

3. American Psychiatric Association, op. cit.

4. Salman Akhtar, *Broken Structures: Severe Personality Disorders and their Treatment* (Northvale, NJ: Jason Aronson, 1992); Richard D. Chessick, *Psychology of the Self and the Treatment of Narcissism* (Northvale, NJ: Jason Aronson, 1985); Otto Kernberg, *Borderline Conditions and Pathological Narcissism* (New York: Jason Aronson, 1975).

5. Ovid, *Metamorphoses*, translated by Frank Justin Miller (1916; reprint, Cambridge, MA: Harvard University Press, 1936), p. 157.
6. Ibid., p. 149.
7. Chessick, op. cit., p. 5.
8. Havelock Ellis, "Auto-Erotism, a Psychological Study," *St. Louis Alienist and Neurologist* 19 (April 1898), as referenced by Jeffrey Berman, *Narcissism and the Novel* (New York: New York University Press, 1990).
9. Paul Nacke, as cited in Elizabeth Wright, ed., *Feminism and Psychoanalysis: A Critical Dictionary* (Oxford, UK: Blackwell Publishers, 1992), p. 271.
10. Sigmund Freud, *"Three Essays on the Theory of Sexuality"* (1905), In *Standard Edition*, vol. 7 (see note 2).
11. Otto Rank, *The Double*, edited and translated by Harry Tucker, Jr. (1914; reprint, New York: New American Library, 1979); Freud, "On Narcissism."
12. Freud, "On Narcissism," p. 73.
13. Ibid.; Margaret S. Mahler, Fred Pine, and Anni Bergman, *The Psychological Birth of the Human Infant* (New York: Basic Books, 1975).
14. Margaret S. Mahler, *On Human Symbiosis and the Vicissitudes of Individuation* (New York: International Universities Press, 1968).
15. Sigmund Freud, *The Standard Edition of the Complete Psychological Works of Sigmund Freud*, 24 vols., edited and translated by James Strachey (London: Hogarth Press, 1953–1974); Mahler, Pine, and Bergman, op. cit.
16. Sheldon Bach, *Narcissistic States and the Therapeutic Process* (Northvale, NJ: Jason Aronson, 1985), p. xi.
17. Hervey M. Cleckley, *The Mask of Sanity* (London: C. V. Mosby Co., 1976).

Chapter 4

1. Alcoholics Anonymous, *Alcoholics Anonymous* (Cornwall, NY: Cornwall Press, 1939).
2. Scott M. Peck, *The Road Less Traveled: A New Psychology of Love, Traditional Values, and Spiritual Growth* (New York: Simon and Schuster, 1978); Ellen Bass and Laura Davis, *The Courage to Heal: A Guide for Women Survivors of Child Sexual Abuse* (New York: Perennial Library, 1990).

Chapter 5

1. Viktor Frankl, *Man's Search for Meaning* (New York: Simon and Schuster, 1963), p. 125.

2. Robert Cohen, *Communications Workshop*, seminar given at Washington County Community Mental Health Center, Charlestown, RI, 1985.
3. John Bradshaw, *Healing the Shame That Binds You* (Deerfield Beach, FL: Health Communications, 1988).
4. Herbert Benson with Miriam Klipper, *The Relaxation Response* (New York: Avon Books, 1975).
5. Oscar Buros, *Mental Measurements Yearbook* (Highland Park, NJ: Gryphon Press, 1990).
6. George R. Bach, *The Intimate Enemy: How to Fight Fair in Love and Marriage* (New York: William Morrow, 1969).

Chapter 6

1. Marion F. Soloman, *Narcissism and Intimacy: Love and Marriage in an Age of Confusion* (New York: W. W. Norton, 1989).
2. Terry Kellogg, *Finding Balance: 12 Priorities for Interdependence and Joyful Living* (Deerfield Beach, FL: Health Communications, 1991), p. 192.
3. Eric Berne, *Games People Play* (New York: Grove Press, 1964).

Chapter 7

1. Ernest Tubb, "Tomorrow Never Comes," recorded by Elvis Presley in album *I'm 10,000 Years Old* on RCA label.
2. Carl Jung, "Archetypes of the Unconscious," as referenced in Marion Woodman, *Addiction to Perfection: The Still Unravished Bride* (Toronto: Inner City Books, 1982), p. 25.
3. Hilde Bruche, *Eating Disorders: Obesity, Anorexia Nervosa, and the Person Within* (New York: Basic Books, 1973).
4. 20th Century-Fox Film Corporation, *An Unmarried Woman*, video recording (Farmington Hills, MI: Magnetic Video Corp., 1978).

Chapter 8

1. Ovid, *Metamorphoses*, as referenced in Jeffrey Berman, *Narcissism and the Novel* (New York: New York University Press, 1990), p. 7.
2. American Psychiatric Association, *Diagnostic and Statistical Manual of Mental Disorders*, revised 3rd ed. (Washington, DC: American Psychiatric Association, 1987); Eliana Gil, *Treatment of Adult Survivors of Childhood Abuse* (Walnut Creek, CA: Launch Press, 1988).
3. American Psychiatric Association, op. cit., Eliana Gil, op. cit.
4. Christine A. Courtois, *Healing the Incest Wound: Adult Survivors in Therapy* (New York: W.W. Norton, 1988).

5. Ernest R. Hilgard, *Divided Consciousness: Multiple Controls in Human Thought and Action* (New York: John Wiley & Sons, 1977); William James, *Principals of Psychology* (1890; reprint, New York: DE: Dover Reprints, 1950).
6. Hilde Bruche, *Eating Disorders: Obesity, Anorexia Nervosa, and the Person Within* (New York: Basic Books, 1973).
7. American Psychiatric Association, op. cit., Courtois, op. cit.

Chapter 9

1. Eileen Gouge, *Such Devoted Sisters* (New York: Viking Press, 1992).
2. Janet G. Woititz, *Adult Children of Alcoholics*, expanded version (Deerfield Beach, FL: Health Communications, 1990).
3. Eliana Gil, *Outgrowing the Pain: A Book for and About Adults Abused as Children* (New York: Dell, 1988).
4. Robert Frost, "The Mending Wall," in *The Poetry of Robert Frost*, edited by Edward Connery Lathem (New York: Rinehart & Winston, 1969).

Appendix A

1. Sigmund Freud, "On Narcissism: An Introduction," in *The Standard Edition of the Complete Psychological Works of Sigmund Freud*, vol. 14, edited and translated by James Strachey (1914; reprint, London: Hogarth Press, 1953–1974), p. 75.
2. Ibid.
3. Ibid.
4. Ibid.
5. Ibid., p. 89.
6. Ibid.
7. Ibid.
8. Ibid., p. 91.
9. Melanie Klein, *Envy and Gratitude and Other Works, 1946–1963* (London: Virago, 1988); Heinz Kohut, *Self Psychology and the Humanities: Reflections on a New Psychonalytic Approach*, edited by Charles B. Strozier (New York: W.W. Norton, 1985).
10. Heinz Kohut, *The Analysis of the Self* (New York: International Universities Press, 1971); Otto Kernberg, *Borderline Conditions and Pathological Narcissism* (New York: Jason Aronson, 1975).
11. D. W. Winnicott, "Transitional Objects and Transitional Phenomena," *International Journal of Psycho-Analysis* 34 (1953): 89–97.
12. Heinz Kohut, *The Search for the Self*, 2 vols., edited by Paul H. Ornstein (New York: International Universities Press, 1978).

13. Sigmund Freud, "Introductory Lectures on Psycho-Analysis" (1916–1917). In *Standard Edition*, vol. 16 (see note 1).

14. Kohut, *The Search for the Self*; Heinz Kohut, *How Does Psychoanalysis Cure?* edited by Arnold Goldberg (Chicago: University of Chicago Press, 1984).

15. Klein, op. cit.; W.R.D. Fairbairn, *An Object Relations Theory of the Personality* (New York: Basic Books, 1952); Harry Guntrip, *Personality Structure and Human Interaction* (New York: International Universities Press, 1961); Winnicott, op. cit.; D. W. Winnicott, *Maturational Processes and the Facilitating Environment* (New York: International Universities Press, 1965).

16. Margaret S. Mahler, Fred Pine, and Anni Bergman, *The Psychological Birth of the Human Infant* (New York: Basic Books, 1975).

17. Mahler, Pine, and Bergman, op. cit.

18. Freud, "On Narcissism: an Introduction."

19. Margaret S. Mahler, *On Human Symbiosis and the Vicissitudes of Individuation* (New York: International Universities Press, 1968).

20. Mahler, Pine, and Bergman, op. cit.

21. Akhtar, op. cit.

22. Sophie Freud, "Overloving and Underloving," in *The Yearbook of Psychoanalysis and Psychotherapy*, edited by Robert Langs (New York: Gardner Press, 1987).

23. Otto Kernberg, *Borderline Conditions and Pathological Narcissism* (New York: Jason Aronson, 1975).

24. Otto Kernberg, "Hysterical and Histrionic Personality Disorders," In *Psychiatry*, vol. 1, edited by R. Michels and J. O. Cavenar Jr., Philadelphia: Lippincott, 1985), pp. 1–12.

25. Kernberg, *Borderline Conditions and Pathological Narcissism*.

26. Otto Kernberg, "Factors in the Treatment of Narcissistic Personality Disorder," *Journal of the American Psychoanalytic Association* 18 (1980): 51–85.

27. Kernberg, *Borderline Conditions and Pathological Narcissism*; Kernberg, "Factors in the Treatment of Narcissistic Personality Disorder."

28. Jeffrey Berman, *Narcissism and the Novel* (New York: New York University Press, 1990).

29. Otto Kernberg, *Internal World and External Reality* (New York: Jason Aronson, 1980), cited in Salman Akhtar, *Broken Structures: Severe Personality Disorders and Their Treatment* (Northvale, NJ: Jason Aronson, 1992), p. 138.

30. Kernberg, *Internal World and External Reality*.

31. Richard D. Chessick, *Psychology of the Self and the Treatment of Narcissism* (Northvale, NJ: Jason Aronson, 1985).

32. Berman, op. cit., p. 26.

33. Chessick, op. cit., p. 232.

34. Kohut, *The Analysis of Self*.
35. Chessick, op. cit.
36. Kohut, *The Search for the Self*.
37. Carl G. Jung, *The Collected Works* (Bollinger Series), 20 vols., translated by R.F.C. Hull and edited by H. Read et al. (Princeton, NJ: Princeton University Press, 1953–1979).
38. Heinz Kohut, *The Restoration of the Self* (New York: International Universities Press, 1977), p. 243.
39. Chessick, op. cit., p. 232.
40. Sheldon Bach, "On Narcissistic State of Consciousness." *International Journal of Psycho-Analysis* 58(1977):209–233.
41. Akhtar, *Broken Structures*.
42. A. M. Cooper, "The Narcissistic-Masochistic Character," in *Masochism: Current Psychoanalytic Perspectives*, edited by R. A. Glick and D. I. Meyers (Hillsdale, NJ: Analytic Press, 1988), as referenced in Akhtar, op. cit.
43. Robert Stolorow and Frank M. Lachmann, *Psychoanalysis of Developmental Arrest* (New York: Universities Press, 1980).
44. Kohut, *The Search for the Self*.
45. Bach, "On Narcissistic State of Consciousness."
46. Roy F. Baumeister, *Masochism and the Self* (Hillsdale, New Jersey: Lawrence Erlbaum Associates, 1989).
47. Freud, "On Narcissism: An Introduction."
48. American Psychiatric Association, *Diagnostic and Statistical Manual of Mental Disorders*, revised 3rd ed. Washington, DC: American Psychiatric Association, 1987).
49. Chessick, op. cit.

Bibliography

Alcoholics Anonymous. *Alcoholics Anonymous*. Cornwall, NY: Cornwall Press, 1939.

Akhtar, Salman. *Broken Structures: Severe Personality Disorders and Their Treatment*. Northvale, NJ: Jason Aronson, 1992.

American Psychiatric Association. *Diagnostic and Statistical Manual of Mental Disorders*, revised 3rd ed. Washington, DC: Author, 1987.

Baumeister, Roy F. *Masochism and the Self*. Hillsdale, NJ: Lawrence Erlbaum Associates, 1989.

Bach, George R. *The Intimate Enemy: How to Fight Fair in Love and Marriage*. New York: William Morrow, 1969.

Bach, Sheldon. "On Narcissistic State of Consciousness." *International Journal of Psychoanalysis* 58(1977):209–233.

Bach, Sheldon. *Narcissistic States and the Therapeutic Process*. Northvale, NJ: Jason Aronson, 1985.

Bass, Ellen, and Laura Davis. *The Courage to Heal: A Guide for Women Survivors of Child Sexual Abuse*. New York: Perennial Library, 1990.

Benson, Herbert, with Miriam Klipper. *The Relaxation Response*. New York: Avon Books, 1975.

Berne, Eric. *Games People Play*. New York: Grove Press, 1964.

Bergmann, Martin S. "The Legend of Narcissus." *American Imago* 41 (1984): 389–411.

Berman, Jeffrey. *Narcissism and the Novel*. New York: New York University Press, 1990.

Black, Claudia. *It Will Never Happen to Me.* Denver, CO: MAC Printing and Publications, 1982.

Bradshaw, John. *Healing the Shame That Binds You.* Deerfield Beach, FL: Health Communications, 1988.

Bruche, Hilde. *Eating Disorders: Obesity, Anorexia Nervosa, and the Person Within.* New York: Basic Books, 1973.

Bruche, Hilde. *Learning Psychotherapy: Rationale and Ground Rules.* Cambridge, MA: Harvard University Press, 1974.

Buros, Oscar. *Mental Measurements Yearbook* (published annually). Highland Park, NJ: Gryphon Press, 1990.

Chessick, Richard D. *Psychology of the Self and the Treatment of Narcissism.* Northvale, NJ: Jason Aronson, 1985.

Cleckley, Hervey M. *The Mask of Sanity.* London: C. V. Mosby Company, 1976.

Cohen, Robert, *Communications Workshop.* Seminar given at Washington County Community Mental Health Center, Charlestown, RI, 1985, unpublished.

Cooper, A. M. "The Narcissistic-Masochistic Character." In *Masochism: Current Psychoanalytic Perspectives*, edited by R. A. Glick and D. I. Meyers. Hillsdale, NJ: Analytic Press, 1988.

Courtois, Christine A. *Healing the Incest Wound: Adult Survivors in Therapy.* New York: W. W. Norton, 1988.

Ellis, Havelock. "Auto-Erotism, a Psychological Study." *St. Louisville Alienist and Neurologist* 19 (April 1898).

Erikson, E. H. *Identity: Youth and Crisis.* New York: W. W. Norton, 1968.

Fairbairn, W. R. D. *An Object Relations Theory of the Personality.* New York: Basic Books, 1952.

Fine, Reuben. *Narcissism, the Self, and Society.* New York: Columbia University Press, 1986.

Guntrip, Harry, *Personality Structure and Human Interaction.* New York: International Universities Press, 1961.

Frankl, Viktor. *Man's Search for Meaning.* New York: Simon and Schuster, 1962.

Freud, Sigmund. *The Standard Edition of the Complete Psychological Works of Sigmund Freud*, 24 vols., edited and translated by James Strachey London: Hogarth Press, 1953–1974.

Freud, Sophie. "Overloving and Underloving." In *The Yearbook of Psychoanalysis and Psychotherapy*, edited by Robert Langs. New York: Gardner Press, 1987.

Frost, Robert. "The Mending Wall" In *The Poetry of Robert Frost*, edited by Edward Connery Lathem. New York: Rinehart & Winston, 1969.

Gil, Eliana. *Outgrowing the Pain: A Book for and About Adults Abused as Children.* New York: Dell, 1988.

Gil, Eliana. *Treatment of Adult Survivors of Childhood Abuse*, Walnut Creek, CA: Launch Press, 1988.

Gouge, Eileen, *Such Devoted Sisters*. New York: Viking Press, 1992.

Grubman-Black, Steven. *Broken Boys/Mending Men*. New York: Ivy Books, 1992.

Hilgard, Ernest, R. *Divided Consciousness: Multiple Controls in Human Thought and Action*, New York: John Wiley & Sons, 1977.

James, William. *Principals of Psychology*. New York: Dover Reprints, 1950 (original, 1890).

Jung, Carl G. *The Collected Works* (Bollinger Series), 20 vols., translated by R.F.C. Hull and edited by H. Read et al. Princeton, NJ: Princeton University Press, 1953-1979.

Kellogg, Terry. *Finding Balance: 12 Priorities for Interdependence and Joyful Living*. Deerfield Beach, FL: Health Communications, 1991.

Kernberg, Otto. *Borderline Conditions and Pathological Narcissism*. New York: Jason Aronson, 1975.

Kernberg, Otto. "Hysterical and Histrionic Personality Disorders." In *Psychiatry*, vol. 1, edited by J. O. Cavenar, Jr., Philadelphia: Lippincott; 1985, pp. 1-12.

Kernberg, Otto. *Internal World and External Reality*. New York: Jason Aronson, 1980.

Klein, Melanie. *Envy and Gratitude and Other Works, 1946-1963*. London: Virago, 1988.

Klein, Melanie. *The Psycho-Analysis of Children*. London: Virago, 1989.

Kohut, Heinz. *The Analysis of Self*. New York: International Universities Press, 1971.

Kohut, Heinz. *How Does Psychoanalysis Cure?* edited by Arnold Goldberg. Chicago: University of Chicago Press, 1984.

Kohut, Heinz. *The Restoration of the Self*. New York: International Universities Press, 1977.

Kohut, Heinz. *The Search for the Self*, 2 vols., edited by Paul H. Ornstein. New York: International Universities Press, 1978.

Kohut, Heinz. *Self Psychology and the Humanities: Reflections on a New Psychoanalytic Approach*, edited by Charles B. Strozier. New York: W. W. Norton, 1985.

Lacan, Jacques. *The Seminar of Jacques Lacan*, 2 vols., edited by Alan Miller and translated by John Forester. Cambridge, UK: Cambridge University Press, 1988.

Mahler, Margaret S. *On Human Symbiosis and the Vicissitudes of Individuation*. New York: International Universities Press, 1968.

Mahler, Margaret S. Fred Pine, and Anni Bergman. *The Psychological Birth of the Human Infant*. New York: Basic Books, 1975.

Maslow, A. H. *Toward a Psychology of Being*. New York: Van Nostrand, 1962.

Mayer, Adele. *Incest: A Treatment Manual for Therapy with Victims, Spouses and Offenders*. Holmes Beach, FL: Learning Publications, 1983.

Ovid. *Metamorphoses*, translated by Frank Justin Miller. Cambridge, MA: Harvard University Press, 1936.

Peck, Scott M. *The Road Less Travelled: A New Psychology of Love, Traditional Values, and Spiritual Growth*. New York: Simon and Schuster, 1978.

Rank, Otto. *The Double*, edited and translated by Harry Tucker, Jr. New York: New American Library, 1979.

Robinson, Bryan E. *Working with Children of Alcoholics: The Practitioner's Handbook*. Lexington, MA: Lexington Books, 1989.

Sandler, Joseph, et al. *Freud's "On Narcissism: An Introduction"*. New Haven, CT: Yale University Press, 1991.

Soloman, Marion F. *Narcissism and Intimacy: Love and Marriage in an Age of Confusion*. New York: W. W. Norton Company, 1989.

Stolorow, Robert, and Frank M. Lachmann, *Psychoanalysis of Developmental Arrest*, New York: Universities Press, 1980.

20th Century-Fox Film Corporation. *An Unmarried Woman*, video recording. Farmington Hills, MI: Magnetic Video Corp., 1978.

20th Century-Fox Film Corporation. *The King and I*, remastered video recording. New York: CBS Fox Video, 1991.

Tubb, Ernest. "Tomorrow Never Comes." Recorded by Elvis Presley in album *I'm 10,000 Years Old* on RCA label.

Winnicott, D. W. *Maturational Processes and the Facilitating Environment*. New York: International Universities Press, 1965.

Winnicott, D. W. "Transitional Objects and Transitional Phenomena." *International Journal of Psycho-Analysis* 34 (1953): 89–97.

Woititz, Janet G. *Adult Children of Alcoholics*, expanded version. Deerfield Beach, FL: Health Communications, 1990.

Woodman, Marion. *Addiction to Perfection: The Still Unravished Bride*. Toronto: Inner City Books, 1982.

Wolpe, J. *The Practice of Behavioral Therapy*, 2nd ed. New York: Paragon Press, 1973.

Wright, Elizabeth, ed. *Feminism and Psychoanalysis: A Critical Dictionary*. Oxford, UK: Blackwell Publishers, 1992.

Index

About the Authors

Stephanie Donaldson-Pressman, M.S.W., whose background is in clinical social work, is a therapist, consultant, and author. Most of her therapeutic work is with adults who have grown up in severely dysfunctional families. She is particularly known for her work with survivors of incest. As a consultant, she has assisted both industrial and church organizations in implementing gender issues workshops and sexual abuse prevention programs.

Robert M. Pressman, Ph.D., is the director of the Rhode Island Psychological Center and is probably best known for his successful books about management of clinical practice. He is a diplomate of the American Board of Professional Psychology (Family Psychology Division). He has been in clinical practice for over twenty years.